CAMPION

CAMPION

A Play in Two Acts

BY
Christopher Buckley
AND
James MacGuire

IGNATIUS PRESS   SAN FRANCISCO

Cover by Christopher J. Pelicano

© 1990 Christopher Buckley and James MacGuire
All rights reserved
ISBN 0–89870–285–2
Library of Congress catalogue number 89–83262
Printed in the United States of America

To the memory of

Rev. Ignacio Ellacuría
Rev. Ignacio Martín-Baro
Rev. Segundo Montes
Rev. Joaquín López y López
Rev. Amando López
Rev. Juan Ramón Moreno
of the Society of Jesus

Murdered in El Salvador,
November 16, 1989

"Our hopes are likewise increasing for the future reunion of the separated members of the one mystical body of Christ, in the knowledge that we have in heaven such allies and representatives of the cause of union and peace among all Christians."

> — Pope Paul VI on the occasion of the canonization of Edmund Campion, Alexander Briant, Ralph Sherwin, and thirty-seven others on October 25, 1970.

Contents

Preface

This is a true story.

For all its splendor, sixteenth-century England was a time of violent religious and social upheaval. It began in 1534, when Henry VIII broke with the Church of Rome over his divorce from Catherine of Aragon and subsequent marriage to Anne Boleyn. A separate, Anglican church was formed with Henry as its Supreme Head; the old Church was suppressed, and its property—then consisting of some 30 percent of all England—was confiscated. Many martyrs to the old religion died in conditions of unspeakable cruelty. The best known among them, Thomas More, was spared the gruesome execution meted out to most of the English Catholics convicted of treason on account of their Faith: They were hanged, cut down while still alive, drawn, and quartered.

After the brief but intensely reforming regime of Edward VI, the throne passed in 1553 to Henry's daughter by his first marriage, Mary. She was a devout, even fanatical Catholic, who restored the ancient Faith, but who also ushered in another era of ghastly persecutions, this time against Protestant dissenters of sincere conviction.

Queen Mary died in 1558 and was succeeded
by Queen Elizabeth, Henry's daughter by Anne
Boleyn. Elizabeth had been raised a Protestant,
and it was under her reign that the Church of
England was restored as the state religion, and
so it has remained for over four hundred years.
Catholicism was once again banned; severe fines
were levied against the "recusants", those who
refused to attend the Anglican services; Catholic
priests were put to death.

Campion takes place between 1566 and 1581,
the middle years of Elizabeth's reign. With the
exchequer bankrupted by her father and with ag-
gressive Catholic neighbors challenging her very
legitimacy, it was natural for the Queen to be
wary. She was not unsympathetic to the Catholic
Faith and was known to enjoy the Latin service,
which had been outlawed during her half-brother
Edward's reign. The pressures on her to suppress
Catholicism for political reasons were great, however, and the prevailing atmosphere was nearly
always treacherous. Henry had created a whole
new landed aristocracy with his grants of the
suppressed monastic lands, and these families,
which included the Cecils (the forebears of her
Secretary of State), were not of a mind to give
anything back. In this world, religion *was* politics,
no matter how hard Catholics strove to separate
the two.

Edmund Campion had been born to a family in

London. His father was a bookseller. His parents
were both dead by the time he was ordained as a
Jesuit. He had two brothers, of whom little is
known. A sister enters the story (although not our
play) when she visits him after his sentence has
been passed down to assure him that there is yet
time for him to repudiate his beliefs and gain
mercy. Campion went to a good grammar school
and obtained a scholarship to study at Christ's
Hospital, Newgate Street. It was while a student
here that he was chosen from among all the schoolboys of London to address Mary Tudor in Latin
from a street platform under the shadow of Old
St. Paul's Cathedral as the Queen, having just
succeeded to the throne, entered the City in state.
Her younger half-sister, the Lady Elizabeth, was
there on that occasion. From Christ's Hospital
Campion went up to Oxford in 1555. At Mary
Tudor's death Elizabeth ascended the throne, restored the Protestant religion and banned Roman
Catholicism once more. This was the start of the
ambitious young Campion's dilemma, and with
Elizabeth's visit to Oxford we begin our play.

Edmund Campion believed himself as loyal to
the sovereign as any Englishman. His relationship
to the Queen is historical. It was long and warm.
Their final furtive meeting and attempt to come to
terms did in fact take place. The Queen wanted to
assist him. However, in the climate of the time it

was inevitable that Elizabeth's ministers would have succeeded in portraying Campion as something else—an insurrectionist, the vanguard of the Spanish Armada.

Campion knew how he would be received, but he embraced his mission nonetheless. Having struggled to reach what he saw as the Truth, he could not turn his back to it and was obedient to his conscience even at the terrible cost of the ordeal that would lead to his death. He was not alone. The list of the English and Welsh martyrs who gave their lives for the Faith between 1535 and 1680 numbers almost four hundred. Most of them suffered the same execution that Campion did, but it is no dishonor to them to say that few of them gave up as much as he.

As the similarity in subject has been remarked upon we would like to express our great admiration for Robert Bolt's magnificent play, *A Man for All Seasons*. We first read the play and saw the film while classmates at Portsmouth Abbey School in Rhode Island nearly twenty-five years ago, and it made a profound impression on us both. However, our aim in writing *Campion* was not to imitate Mr. Bolt. In fact the spark which first inspired this play was watching a rerun of *Brideshead Revisited* and realizing, for the first time, that it was the story of one man's conversion. That led to a renewed interest in the story of the English recusants, and that, in time, led us to Edmund Campion. In writing the play we took care to adopt a different production approach from that which Mr. Bolt had employed. Also, it seemed to us that the stories were fundamentally different. For one thing, More was a mature and powerful man at the time of his crisis, and until the last he hoped to avoid the fate that was to be his. Campion, on the other hand, felt compelled to give up his worldly ambitions at an early age and thereafter spent his life in preparation for the martyrdom he knew would follow if ever his wish to reenter England were granted. Secondly, there is an intangible difference in the More/Henry, Campion/Elizabeth conflicts. They are both fascinating confrontations, but there is a subtle, sexual undertone to the meeting of Campion and Elizabeth.

We are indebted to Dom Julian Stead, O.S.B., and the Honorable Georgina Stonor for their assistance as we embarked on this enterprise. Among many other sources (see bibliography), we have relied heavily on Evelyn Waugh's *Edmund Campion, Jesuit and Martyr*. Some of the dialogue was actually spoken and written by Edmund Campion. We hope that it will reflect more on his genius and grace than our lack of them, that his words stand

out clearly—generous, luminous, and wise—from
the troubled age it was his special glory to inhabit
down to our own.

Christopher Buckley, Washington, D.C.
James MacGuire, New York City

April, 1990

The world premiere of *Campion* was presented on June 23, 1987, by the Williamstown Theatre Festival, the late Nikos Psacharopoulos, Artistic Director.

Directed by Kevin Kelley.

The Original Cast

CAMPION . . . . Harry Groener

ELIZABETH . . . . Laurie Kennedy

CECIL . . . . Paul Collins

WALSINGHAM . . . . Kenneth Tigar

LEICESTER . . . . Tom Tammi

D'ALENÇON . . . . Howard Samuelson

ALLEN . . . . Tom Brennan

Notes on the Major Characters

EDMUND CAMPION is twenty-six at the beginning of the play and forty-one at its end. He wears a beard without which he might look ten years younger. Has a handsome face that can sometimes look slightly gaunt and intense eyes. Has a radiant personality, which by all contemporary accounts was possessed of an enormous and even mysterious inner gaiety. One of the most charismatic men of the age. Oddly relaxed in the royal presence. His smile comes readily, even in the midst of physical trial.

ELIZABETH, QUEEN OF ENGLAND. In the middle years of her reign. Quick-tempered and -witted, she is capable of veering from girlish teasing to towering tantrums without ever losing absolute control. Her great triumph over the Armada is still years off, but she is every inch the Queen, confident in power and accustomed to rule.

WILLIAM CECIL, FIRST BARON BURGHLEY. Sixtyish. Has tall, high forehead; white beard; blue, suspicious eyes. Elizabeth's first minister and Secretary of State. The Queen's favorite counselor. Conservative, dispassionate, ruthless in the preservation of the new order.

SIR FRANCIS WALSINGHAM. Principal secretary to Elizabeth and head of her secret service. Late forties. Dark, stout, menacing, Puritan. The only man Elizabeth is said to fear. Behind his back she calls him "the Moor". A man of great vision and small humanity.

ROBERT DUDLEY, EARL OF LEICESTER. Late forties. Past hope of marrying Elizabeth, he nonetheless remains "Sweet Robin" to her, and he tries to curry favor as assiduously as the Queen will permit. Flamboyant, high-spirited, generous, haughty. Incapable of understanding sacrifice unless it is for worldly glory, he is impatient with and puzzled by Campion's obduracy.

DOCTOR WILLIAM ALLEN. Eventually the last of the great English cardinal-politicians. Late forties. Physically and mentally robust despite his anguish at sending so many of his seminarians to their deaths on the English Mission. Revered by his students. After the martyrs themselves, the man most responsible for the survival of Catholicism in England.

Production Notes

Campion is an episodic, free-flowing drama conceived in the style of *Nicholas Nickelby* or Tony Harrison's *The Mysteries*, as opposed to a static, drawing-room piece. It is important to link the play to its time via the production approach. That is, the play takes place between 1566 and 1581, at the dawn of the Elizabethan stage. It also looks back to the great pillars of fourteenth- and fifteenth-century drama, the mystery plays, and other church-sponsored drama.

At Williamstown a second stage was constructed above and toward the rear of the first one, with stairs leading up at stage right. At stage left was a spiral staircase, concealed from the audience by a black curtain. The upper stage was constructed entirely of metal, the harsh sounds emanating from which were meant to convey the dangers and treacheries of the Elizabethan era. The authors are open to other design solutions.

"English" English is preferred to mid-Atlantic speech not only because it is more authentic but also because it creates opportunities for humor in the regional (Cockney, Lancashire, West Country, East Anglian, and so on) dialects of the minor characters. Music is an important element in the play. While on the whole the music should be faithful to the period, a song or dance could be staged to an appropriate folk rock song.

As to costumes, Elizabeth wears a red wig and suitably royal attire. Campion starts out in the dress of a poor scholar. In the first court scene he is slightly more prosperously attired. After he flees, he is clothed as a priest until he returns to England, at which point his disguise is that of an extravagant, dandified gentleman. Cecil has a staff of office. Walsingham is dressed in black. Leicester is flamboyant but stylish. D'Alençon is flamboyant and ridiculous.

Major Characters

Edmund Campion
Elizabeth, Queen of England
William Cecil, Baron Burghley
Sir Francis Walsingham
Robert Dudley, Earl of Leicester
Dr. William Allen

Also, various Catholic squires, courtiers, students, priest hunters, jailer, guards, bailiff, Queen's Counsel, torturers, jury, and so on.

Act One

1566–1581
England, the Low Countries, Rome, and Prague

Act Two

July–December 1581
The Tower of London, Richmond Palace,
Westminster Hall, and Tyburn

ACT ONE

Prologue

Dark stage. As the house lights dim, a figure runs down the aisle, bounds up onto the stage, and disappears. He is followed by others, carrying torches and weapons. Sounds of a violent house search. Banging on panels, splintering of wood. Voices *cry out.*

VOICE There's no one here.

SECOND VOICE Damn you! He is here. He said Mass here hours ago. I was there. Keep searching.

VOICE [*Grumbling*] There's no one here, I tell you. Tear the whole place down for all I care.

SECOND VOICE This search will continue, or you shall explain why before the Privy Council.

[*The fugitive has been inching his way across the back of the stage, barely discernible.*]

THIRD VOICE There, by the stairs!

[*The fugitive flees, but the men close to pounce on him just offstage. A cry is heard. Stage black.*]

Scene One

Music suitable for a royal procession. Lights up. Characters frozen. Campion, *standing, is addressing* Elizabeth *and her court, consisting of* Cecil, Walsingham, Leicester, *and various courtiers, seated.* Young Man *appears at stage right.*

YOUNG MAN   In the summer of 1556 Her Royal Highness, Queen Elizabeth, paid a visit to Oxford. It was primarily a recruiting mission. The ranks of the Anglican churchmen had been thinned by her Catholic half-sister, Queen Mary. In her short reign Bloody Mary had burned over three hundred Protestants at the stake. Now, under Good Queen Bess, the state religion was once again Protestant, Catholic priests were on the run, and Elizabeth was determined to have the best and the brightest for *her* clergy. The Earl of Leicester, the Queen's ardent admirer, had among his titles that of Chancellor of the University. He arranged for Elizabeth to see Oxford's finest minds in action.

The most brilliant scholar of the day was Edmund Campion, so popular that the students were said to follow him in the streets, imitating the way he walked. Leicester called on him to improvise a speech in the royal presence.

CAMPION   *Ignem veni mittere in terram.* I have come
to send fire on the earth, and what will I if it be
already kindled? The disciples felt that fire themselves, in the form of a tongue of flame. They
had gathered secretly in the Upper Room, alone,
terrified, and fugitive. Bleak night was closing
in. Their tormentors were in the streets outside.

That night might have marked the end of the
Church. But then something happened, something marvelous strange: the hot breath of the
Holy Ghost, kindling the fire that has burned
brightly for fifteen centuries.

What Prometheus had to steal from the gods
of pagan antiquity—a crime for which he paid
most horrible, his liver ripped out and eaten
every day by the terrible eagle—the Christian
God gives freely. And man, alas, uses not always wisely. Or to evil ends. In our own time,
in our own country, fire has been put to ghastly
use. The embers of Smithfield, where hundreds
perished, are yet warm.

England might have perished with the Protestant martyrs. Yet she did not. For out of those
ashes has come a great ruler, Elizabeth, our
Queen, wise and beautiful, learned and just.
She has been praised in verse of every meter and
likened to the goddess Diana, a great huntress
who seeks out men's hearts and conquers them.

"And what will I if I already be kindled?"

Now bonfires blaze on every hill, like the fire crosses that summoned the ancient clans to battle. The darkness is banished, and all Albion is aflame with her spirit! She is the spark—

COURTIERS   Hear, hear!

CAMPION   [*Voice rising*] —inspiring us to greatness—

COURTIERS   Hear, hear!

CAMPION   —and now all England is on [*Shouts*] fire!

[*The Courtiers cheer and applaud. Campion bows to Elizabeth, who beams. Leicester claps Campion on the back. Two men burst in, spilling buckets of water. The Courtiers, seeing this, laugh heartily.*]

ELIZABETH   [*Laughing*] If you've come to put out the fire, there [*Pointing to Campion*] he is. [*More laughter*] Leicester.

LEICESTER   Majesty.

[*Leicester nods to Campion, who walks forward and kneels in front of Elizabeth.*]

CAMPION   Her Majesty does Oxford great honor.

ELIZABETH   We would have come last year but for the plague. You have spoken well, Master Campion.

CAMPION   I was well inspired, speaking in the

name of Philosophy, the Princess of letters, before Elizabeth, the lettered Princess.

[*Elizabeth, preening, removes a ring and gives it to Campion, still kneeling. Campion bows his head.*]

ELIZABETH   Rise, our gifted young scholar. [*He does*] You are deacon already, are you not?

CAMPION   Yes, Majesty.

ELIZABETH   Splendid. Then you may come and preach to us. [*Impressed looks among the Courtiers. A scowl from Walsingham*] On your way to Canterbury. [*Campion bows*] Come, Cecil, we wish to hear the new translations from the Hebrew. [*Exits*]

CECIL   [*To Leicester*] Six days of strutting scholars. Three would have been sufficient. [*Exits*]

LEICESTER   A formidable man, the Secretary of State. [*Brightly*] So, now you have the Queen's favor.

CAMPION   I am overwhelmed, my lord. It would not have happened without your intercession.

LEICESTER   [*Enjoying himself*] You're a man with a future.

CAMPION   [*Coyly*] I had hoped to have a future.

LEICESTER   [*Missing it*] You shall have my patronage. I'll send for you when we get to Rycote. Her Majesty is weary of being preached to by tiresome divines. They lack [*Looking for the word*] gaiety. Come to court, Edmund. [*Thinks he's being witty*] Set us on "fire"! [*Starts to exit, chuckling; Campion's laugh is just a bit forced. Leicester throws him a purse*] Here. Buy yourself some suitable clothes. [*Exits*]

[*Campion tosses the bag in the air with joy and exits.*]

Scene Two

The royal court at Rycote, two years later. Early evening. Festive courtly airs. Cecil, Walsingham, Dr. Charke, Campion, various courtiers. Elizabeth enters carrying a crossbow, followed by Leicester.

ELIZABETH   It was *glorious!* Six beautiful harts!

[*All bow.*]

LEICESTER   Your Majesty's aim is as true as any man's! [*He takes the crossbow from her*]

ELIZABETH   "As true"?

LEICESTER   [*Laughs*] Truer. [*Tosses the crossbow to an attendant*]

ELIZABETH   We were well instructed. [*Turns to Campion*] Indeed, Master Campion, did we not have the same tutor?

CAMPION   We did, your Majesty. Doctor Ascham. But my curriculum did not include archery. He knew from the start I was a dull scholar, so we concentrated on Cicero.

CHARKE   [*Looking for his opening*] Cicero is admirable enough, but hardly sufficient to ground a man in the classics. Why, by the time I was six years old, I had already exhausted Cicero.

ELIZABETH   Whereas, Doctor Charke, it has only taken you six hours to exhaust us. Indeed, Edmund, we thought your sermon to us this afternoon rather . . . Ciceronian.

CAMPION   Her Majesty exaggerates. As Doctor Charke no doubt recalls, the saying went, "When Seneca speaks, the men say, 'How well he speaks'. But when Cicero speaks, the men say . . .

ELIZABETH and CAMPION   'Let us march'."

[*They laugh. Elizabeth shoots a withering glance at Charke, takes Campion by the arm, and they "march" across stage. She sits on bench and invites him to sit beside her.*]

ELIZABETH   Charke. He drives me to distraction.

CAMPION   He's . . . earnest.

ELIZABETH   He is that.

CAMPION   And one of the brightest lights in Her Majesty's Anglican church.

ELIZABETH   That is precisely the problem with our church.

CAMPION   [*Laughing*] Do I gather Her Majesty's esteem for theologians is not high?

ELIZABETH   Your powers of deduction are extraordinary. But we have you. [*Pats his hand*] And
we have plans for you.

CAMPION   Perhaps the problem isn't entirely the
theologians.

ELIZABETH   [*Suspiciously*] No. The theology is
sound.

CAMPION   [*Probing*] As long as Her Majesty is
completely satisfied. *Is* she?

ELIZABETH   [*Impatiently, but interested*] Edmund,
we have been over all this before.

[*A servant kneels, offering Elizabeth a tray of food.
She declines. Campion takes a piece of bread, regards
it as if about to make a point, but Elizabeth antici-
pates him and takes it from him.*]

ELIZABETH   This—is a piece of bread. It doesn't
matter how many words you say over it. It
remains—a piece of bread.

CAMPION   [*Points to her throne, upper stage*] That is
Her Majesty's throne. But unless Her Majesty
is present in it, it is—a chair.

ELIZABETH   [*Amused*] You flirt with heresy, Edmund.

CAMPION   One has to understand a doctrine if one
is to spend one's life refuting it.

ELIZABETH   Don't understand it too well. It might be inconvenient. And that would make us most unhappy.

CAMPION   Her Majesty's happiness is my heart's desire.

ELIZABETH   We believe it.

[*The moment hangs there between them, until Leicester bursts forward.*]

LEICESTER   Has Her Majesty given any thought to which of her bears she will pit at the bearbaiting on Tuesday?

ELIZABETH   [*She hasn't*] We have. We think . . . Great Ned.

LEICESTER   An excellent choice! Harry Hunks is tucked up after that last fight.

ELIZABETH   [*Pondering*] What about Sackerson?

LEICESTER   [*Coming into his own*] Possibly. Possibly. He's been a bit sluggish, lately. Still, he does have great tenacity . . .

[*He and Elizabeth exit, talking. Walsingham and Cecil turn toward the audience.*]

WALSINGHAM   [*Dourly*] The earl is making his customary contribution to the intellectual life of the court.

CECIL   He has nothing but himself to offer. It is not enough.

WALSINGHAM   But he has considerable properties. He's certainly land rich, however cash poor. [*Malevolently*] I should have thought that would catch your eye . . . [*Cecil glares at him*] Maybe not. Pity. He tried so hard to make himself eligible.

CECIL   [*Grim mirth*] Yes, but oddly, murdering his wife did not strike Her Majesty as the most . . . graceful way of going about it.

WALSINGHAM   I want a word with the young scholar.

[*Walsingham catches Campion's eye and motions him over. Campion walks to them.*]

CAMPION   My lords.

WALSINGHAM   Mr. Campion, do you not share the earl's passion for bearbaiting?

CAMPION   I try to stay out of the pit, my lord.

CECIL   You are settling in comfortably at court, Campion.

CAMPION   Her Majesty is very gracious. [*Carefully*] As are her ministers.

WALSINGHAM   She seems to enjoy your sermons.

CAMPION   It must be their divinely revealed substance which pleases her, and not my all too human delivery.

WALSINGHAM   [*Heavily*] Whatever. It had gotten to the point where she declared she would no longer listen to sermons. Except during Lent.

CECIL   [*Ironically*] Her Majesty was always a believer in mortification. And Doctor Charke was always eager to provide it. [*Down to business*] Now, Campion, there is one sermon we are all eager to hear you give.

CAMPION   [*Knowing full well*] And what is that, my lord?

WALSINGHAM   Against the Pope.

CAMPION   [*Sidestepping*] Her Majesty has been very tolerant of the old Faith.

WALSINGHAM   [*Disapproving*] Indeed she has.

CECIL   That is hardly the point, is it, Campion?

CAMPION   [*Putting the ball in their court*] What is it exactly that you desire me to say against the Pope?

WALSINGHAM   [*Impatiently, gravely*] That he is the sham Bishop of Rome, anti-Christ, blasphemer, ally of Spain, and enemy of England. You know very well what to say.

CECIL [*Playing the good cop*] Come, Edmund, for a scholar you ask peculiar questions.

CAMPION It's the nature of scholars.

WALSINGHAM As a [*Emphatic*] guest of the court, you should consider asking fewer questions. You are to preach at Saint Paul's Cross at Candlemas.

CAMPION I fear I cannot.

WALSINGHAM [*Glowering*] Why?

CAMPION My duties at Oxford, as proctor. I doubt I could have my arguments for such a sermon prepared until . . . Michaelmas.

CECIL I would have thought that someone who could improvise a speech on "fire" in five minutes would not need eight months to prepare one against Rome.

CAMPION [*Coy*] If it's a matter of urgency, why not have Doctor Charke give it?

CECIL Charke is a . . . competent man. But the occasion and the subject require more than competence.

WALSINGHAM [*Very menacing*] *You* will deliver the sermon at Saint Paul's Cross. Is that understood?

[*Sound of court dancing.*]

CECIL   The entertainment is beginning. Come, Walsingham.

[*They exit. Campion is left alone onstage for a moment, until Charke enters.*]

CAMPION   Not joining in?

CHARKE   I don't think Her Majesty is in a good mood today.

CAMPION   Oh, I wouldn't worry. At least you got her attention.

CHARKE   Is *that* what it was?

CAMPION   Well, now you know where she stands on Cicero.

CHARKE   I couldn't help but overhear your conversation with Cecil and Walsingham.

CAMPION   [*Bemused, with a sweep of his eyes to indicate how huge the room is*] Yes, voices do carry in such a small room as this.

CHARKE   I wouldn't call them theologians. [*Campion doesn't respond*] Of course, as ministers, I suppose they have a certain [*Bitterly*] competence.

CAMPION   No doubt the Queen would agree with you there.

CHARKE   And their loyalty is beyond question. [*Abruptly*] Are you going to give that sermon?

CAMPION   The date seems to be set.

CHARKE   You aren't very enthusiastic. Most deacons I know would give their eyeteeth to preach at Saint Paul's Cross.

CAMPION   Actually, I took the liberty of proposing you in my place.

CHARKE   I heard.

CAMPION   I got the impression they're saving you for something more important.

CHARKE   [*Eagerly*] You did?

CAMPION   There was no mistaking it.

CHARKE   [*Relaxing*] So, *are* you going to give the sermon?

CAMPION   [*Parrying*] Tell me, Doctor Charke, you have a deep understanding of the new church . . .

CHARKE   [*Flattered*] Well . . .

CAMPION   . . . and you've penetrated far into the minds of the Anglican fathers.

CHARKE   Yes, far.

CAMPION   And what did you find there?

CHARKE   [*Sharing his secret*] If I believed them as well as understood them, I'd have an answer for you.

CAMPION   I admire your faculty for separation.

CHARKE   One has to accommodate the times. The state religion's changed three times in the last thirty years. It could again.

CAMPION   Miracles happen.

CHARKE   It wouldn't require any miracle. The Queen might marry. Or die.

CAMPION   [*Emphatically*] God forbid.

CHARKE   [*Backing off*] Oh, God forbid. Certainly, God forbid. Meantime, give Cecil and Walsingham their sermon like a good chap. [*Heartily*] You can do it. *I* did. [*Music and laughter offstage*] Come, we're missing the dancing.

[*Charke begins to exit.*]

CAMPION   You go.

[*Charke exits. Campion remains alone. The music and laughter of the court rise as they reenter in force and resume center stage. There are singing and dancing, a juggler, a fool. The Queen dances with Leicester. Campion, looking on from the side, lays down his fine clothing gently on the ground. He exits. Lights down.*]

Scene Three

Oxford. Campion's room. Night. Campion is packing a few small effects, mostly books.

YOUNG MAN   This is lunacy! Insanity! Madness! You can't do this!

CAMPION   [*Distracted, going through his books*] I'll leave the Boethius, I think. Cumbersome.

YOUNG MAN   [*Pacing*] One sermon. One!

CAMPION   But not the Ariosto. [*He holds two books*] The second volume's the best. [*He stuffs it into his pack*]

YOUNG MAN   You're not listening!

CAMPION   My heavens!

YOUNG MAN   What?

CAMPION   My *Utopia*. It's an original. Been looking everywhere for it. Do you know what I paid for it?

YOUNG MAN   Who *cares* what you paid for it?

CAMPION   [*With a poor man's pride*] A shilling six. Went without meat for three weeks.

YOUNG MAN   [*Throwing up his hands*] Will you listen?

CAMPION   [*Returning to his packing*] I can't help but listen, John. You're shouting.

YOUNG MAN   Then answer!

CAMPION   [*Puts down his book*] We've been through it already.

YOUNG MAN   Not to my satisfaction.

CAMPION   I've explained it in English. Do you want it in Latin?

YOUNG MAN   I want it to make sense.

CAMPION   [*Agreeing*] There is no "sense" to it, John.

YOUNG MAN   Don't tell *me* that.

CAMPION   Faith isn't a matter of logic, and I'm a Catholic, John. It's in my blood. It was passed to me by my father, and from his to him, all the way back to . . . I dare not guess. A Roman slave, I should think, from one of the less fashionable houses. [*Anticipating his objection*] Yes, I assented to the new religion. We all did. We all wanted to make our way in the world. [*Thoughtfully*] You know, I truly thought I could . . . make my private peace with God.

An arrangement. What scares me is that but for Cecil and Walsingham, I might have. [*Wistfully*] I shall miss England though.

YOUNG MAN   You're the Queen's favorite. You call giving that up and leaving England "inconvenient"?

CAMPION   John, listen. Christ said to Peter, "You are Peter, and upon this rock I build my Church." I don't recollect his saying that to Queen Elizabeth—however much I might wish he had.

YOUNG MAN   All right. But why are you being so, so bloody *extreme* about it? Things could always change.

CAMPION   Oh, yes. Doctor Charke, in his infinite wisdom, has already explained that. All I have to do is pray fervently for the Queen to marry a Catholic or die.

YOUNG MAN   You could *convert* her! You're the one man who could do it!

CAMPION   [*With a look to show what dangerous ground this is*] Cecil and Walsingham watch me like hawks. The moment they suspected I was up to something—and it wouldn't take them ten minutes—they'd convert me. To worm's meat.

And anyway, I'm no match for the Queen. She has very definite views.

YOUNG MAN   [*Angrily*] Among them that you're the man she wants to head her church.

CAMPION   The Queen has been good to me, John. I would not deceive her. If ever I resolved to win her over, I would do it openly. I owe her that much.

YOUNG MAN   [*Sees he's lost*] But—what are *we* to do without you?

CAMPION   [*With forced exigence*] You . . . are to study, every bit as hard as if I were still here. Your Greek is appalling, John. [*Young Man turns away, fighting tears; Campion as well; he gives him the* Utopia] Here. I want you to have this.

YOUNG MAN   [*Embarrassed*] No, I couldn't.

CAMPION   [*Placing it in his hands*] Take it. It's a present. From your teacher. Remember me.

[*They embrace. Young Man exits.*]

CAMPION   Don't forget your Greek!

Scene Four

Rome. Three years later. Priest *enters lower stage, right.* Campion *prostrates himself before* Priest.

PRIEST Are you willing to renounce the world, all possessions, and all hope of temporal goods?

CAMPION Yes.

PRIEST Are you ready, if necessary, to beg your bread from door to door for the love of Jesus Christ?

CAMPION Yes.

PRIEST Are you ready to reside in any country and to embrace any employment where your superior may think you to be most useful, to the glory of God and the good of souls?

CAMPION Yes.

PRIEST Do you feel resolved generally to renounce without reserve all those things which men in general love and embrace, and will you attempt and desire, with all your strength, what our Lord Jesus Christ loved and embraced?

CAMPION Yes.

PRIEST   Do you consent to put on the livery of
humiliation worn by him, to suffer as he did,
and for love of him, contempt, calumnies, and
insult?

CAMPION   Yes.

[*Priest exits, Campion following.*]

Scene Five

Outside the palace. Night. Man with furtive air enters, holding scroll of parchment, a Papal Bull with a large black cross, and nails it to post. Two guards rush in, arrest him, and drag him roughly offstage, left.

  Elizabeth enters briskly, upper stage, left, followed by *Walsingham,* Cecil, *and* Leicester.

WALSINGHAM   Shall I continue, Majesty?

ELIZABETH   [*Displeased*] Read.

WALSINGHAM   [*With relish—it serves his purpose*] "She is illegitimate, has violated her coronation oath, deposed her bishops, issued an heretical prayer book, and forbidden her subjects the comfort of the sacraments." [*Clears his throat*] "She is therefore declared excommunicate, and her subjects are hereupon released from moral obedience to her."

ELIZABETH   [*Icy*] How *dare* he.

CECIL   The Pope means war, Ma'am.

ELIZABETH   We *know* that, Cecil.

CECIL   Yet Her Majesty has been reluctant to take measures against English papists.

ELIZABETH   How do you mean, "reluctant"? We've outlawed their Mass. Levied fines. Proscribed their Rosaries, their Virgin Mother. Burned their missals and vestments, stoned their stained glass, and turned their altar stones into cheese presses.

WALSINGHAM   Not enough, apparently.

ELIZABETH   [*Defiant*] Hundreds of Protestants died at the stake during my sister's reign. I'll not start killing Catholics, Walsingham. We do not share your Puritan ardor for settling religious disputes with rope and knife. But, by Jesu, I'll not have the Bishop of Rome publishing this poison against me!

CECIL   Then we must at least increase the fines.

ELIZABETH   [*Bitterly*] Oh, we shall. Instruct Parliament. We can use the revenue.

[*Cecil and Walsingham, slightly behind her, nod at each other.*]

WALSINGHAM   Has Her Majesty given any thought to the priests being sent in secretly from the continent?

ELIZABETH   We have.

CECIL   Doctor Allen has been busy since the Pope

issued the Bull excommunicating you, Ma'am. He calls his school in the Low Countries a "seminary". In fact, it's a pit of snakes.

WALSINGHAM   A training school for Roman spies, infiltrated into England in preparation for the day the Pope and the King of Spain send their navies against us.

LEICESTER   If Allen is recruiting English papists and sending them back in as spies, then surely Her Majesty's course is clear?

CECIL   You propose?

LEICESTER   [*Matter of factly*] Kill him.

CECIL   [*Out of patience*] His seminary is on Spanish soil. He's under the protection of Philip. And murder is not the policy of Her Majesty's government.

LEICESTER   [*Affronted*] Certainly not. I was speaking of assassination.

ELIZABETH   [*Amused*] You are impatient, Sweet Robin.

LEICESTER   [*Preening*] When it comes to your safety, I am the most impatient man in the realm.

[*Cecil and Walsingham exchange dubious glances.*]

WALSINGHAM   [*To Leicester*] Then doubtless it will interest you to know that your own Edmund Campion recently completed his [*Sarcastic*] studies at Allen's seminary.

ELIZABETH   Campion?

WALSINGHAM   [*Acidly*] The earl's protégé, if I remember.

LEICESTER   [*Coldly*] You too respected his scholarship, Walsingham. But I thought he was in Ireland—writing a history of it.

ELIZABETH   A history of Ireland? How dreary.

WALSINGHAM   He *was* in Ireland. The Low Countries, Rome. Very fleet of foot, Mister Campion is. Now he's in Prague. [*He knows this will hurt Elizabeth*] A confessor and playwright—in the court of the Holy Roman Emperor.

ELIZABETH   [*Hurt*] Prague. Perhaps our court was not gay enough.

[*Another furtive glance between Cecil and Walsingham.*]

CECIL   Rejecting Her Majesty was an act of colossal ingratitude on his part.

WALSINGHAM   Repugnant.

LEICESTER   He wasn't "rejecting" Her Majesty. You know it had nothing to do with that. He left that letter explaining—

WALSINGHAM   —his whorish embrace of the blasphemous Roman doctrine. For two years Her

Majesty lavished him with generosity and opportunity. And how did he repay her?

LEICESTER   Oh, Walsingham, honestly. It was a
religious . . . thing. [*He's straying into unfamiliar
turf*] That business of the real presence.

ELIZABETH   [*To herself*] Just a piece of bread.

LEICESTER   Angels dancing on pinheads. Theology's an ass.

ELIZABETH   [*Still in her reverie*] He'd have been
bishop by now. And before long, archbishop.
He gave such beautiful sermons. We lost very
much indeed when Master Campion poped.

CECIL   As a scholar, he had great promise. As a
subject, he was a great disappointment.

ELIZABETH   We trust he will be a great success in
Prague. [*Rises and starts to walk out*] Perhaps
some day he will return to England.

CECIL   That is rather what I fear, Majesty.

ELIZABETH   [*Not listening to him*] And to our favor.
An English diamond deserves an English setting.
[*She stops, turns to Cecil and Walsingham*] Fines
will not suffice. Arrest the priests.

[*She exits, followed by Leicester. Cecil and Walsingham smile at each other, then follow.*]

Scene Six

A courtyard in Prague, later that year. Day. Histrionic music. Campion *is directing three* Actors *on upper stage.*

FIRST ACTOR   "How good it is to obey! Truly . . . Truly . . ." Line?

CAMPION   "Truly, how have I been"—

FIRST ACTOR   "—longing for this pleasure!"

[*Two Actors kneel on cue. Middle Actor forgets. Third Actor nudges him; he kneels.*]

SECOND ACTOR   "Come, let us enter the church and offer our souls and ourselves as a sacrifice to the highest sovereign!"

[*They remain, frozen.*]

CAMPION   [*Applauding*] *Bene! Bene!* [*Turns to audience and motions music to stop; the "orchestra" finishes playing; Actors descend to lower stage*] Bravo, Ludovic! Bravo, Gaspar! Bravo, Petrus! If you do as well tomorrow for the Emperor, he will make you all knights of the Holy Roman Empire. But the last scene still seems to me to lack

sincerity. Ludovic—"How good it is to obey!"
Say it for me.

FIRST ACTOR   "How good it is to obey."

CAMPION   You don't sound convinced.

FIRST ACTOR   [*Shouting*] *"How good it is to obey!"*

[*Campion winces.*]

CAMPION   The way you did it before is good
enough. But when you do say it, imagine that
you've just been released from a terrible bond-
age. That your true freedom lies in placing your
life and soul in the hands of God.

FIRST ACTOR   [*Dubious*] Right. Right! Shall I try it
again?

CAMPION   No, I think you'll be fine. Now Gaspar—"Let us enter the church and offer ourselves as a sacrifice to the highest sovereign."
It's your *life* you're about to give up, not a second helping of meat. The play's about life and
death, man.

SECOND ACTOR   I'm not as used to emperors as
you are, Father Edmund. I may forget my cue
to die.

CAMPION   [*With humor*] Well, Gaspar, if you do,

I'm sure the Emperor will assist you. And I may help him.

FIRST ACTOR [*Taking him aside*] Father, my speech in act one. Do you think you might . . . embellish it? Isn't it a bit short?

CAMPION [*They've been over this before*] Ludovic, our play is six hours long.

FIRST ACTOR Well, if you think it's enough . . .

THIRD ACTOR Father, was I all right. You think I was too—

CAMPION [*Teasing*] Enthusiastic?

THIRD ACTOR [*Aghast*] Enthusiastic?

CAMPION No. Grandiloquent?

THIRD ACTOR [*Sagging*] Grandiloquent?

CAMPION Like an overripe pomegranate!

THIRD ACTOR [*Ready to kill himself*] I—was?

CAMPION [*Laughing heartily*] No, Petrus! You were fine. Never better! [*Clasping him*] This imperial summons has made nervous schoolgirls of you. You have nothing to fear.

FIRST ACTOR Except imperial displeasure.

CAMPION Perform for him as you would for his lowliest subject, and all will be well.

SECOND ACTOR Come, Father. Aren't you just the least bit worried yourself? [*Dreamily*] To have your play put on before an emperor. To be summoned—to court!

CAMPION Yes. [*Almost to himself*] To court. [*Shaking off the memory*] But why should I fear when my play is in your hands? Come, you must be hungry. And if I'm not mistaken, young Petrus here would celebrate his triumph tonight with wine!

[*They start to exit.*]

VOICE Father Edmund!

[*A Priest rushes in holding a letter.*]

PRIEST Father! A letter for you! From Rome!

CAMPION [*To Actors*] Go on. I'll join you.

[*Actors exit in high spirits. Priest hands Campion the letter and remains, peering over his shoulder.*]

CAMPION It's from Doctor Allen!

[*Campion rips the letter open and begins to read it. Then, feeling the eyes over his shoulder, he offers the letter to the Priest in a humorous way. The Priest blushes, retreats, and crosses himself. Campion pales as he finishes reading.*]

CAMPION   Dear God.

PRIEST   What?

CAMPION   [*With horror*] I'm to return to England.

PRIEST   *No!*

[*Campion hands the letter to the Priest, who reads it aloud, with mounting terror.*]

PRIEST   "Our harvest there is already great, but ordinary laborers are not enough. The Pope has at last granted that our own Campion, with his extraordinary gifts of wisdom and grace, should be restored to us."
   What will you do?
   [*Pacing, desperate*] The Emperor will grant you protection. Or intercede with the Pope.
   Edmund, you've got to do something. It's a death warrant.

CAMPION   [*Reciting*] "Are you ready to reside in any country, to embrace any employment where your superior may think you to be most useful, to the glory of God and the good of souls?"

PRIEST   But [*Shudders*] *England*?

[*Lights dim to a spotlight on Campion. Priest exits.*]

Scene Seven

The English college at Douai, the Low Countries. Night. Doctor Allen *enters.*

ALLEN   In your choice of disguises, be inventive. There's more safety in looking ridiculous than plain. Large, feathered hats; rich brocade; silk; fine riding boots—that's the thing. You'll be provided with these when you leave.

CAMPION   [*With humor*] I *will* look ridiculous.

ALLEN   Not in God's eyes.

CAMPION   [*Quoting, amused*] "We are made a spectacle unto God, unto his angels and men."

ALLEN   Avoid the company of heretics. You're returning to minister to persecuted Catholics, not to dispute with Anglicans. And you are forbidden—forbidden absolutely—to involve yourself in questions of state. [*Wags his finger*] No politics, Edmund.

CAMPION   [*Dismissive*] I was never one for that.

ALLEN   And permit no conversation against the Queen in your presence.

CAMPION   [*Angry*] I have *never* permitted conversation against the Queen in my presence.

ALLEN   [*Apologetically*] No, of course. You were
her friend.

CAMPION   [*Emphatically*] Am.

ALLEN   [*Eye to eye*] I pray that she might. [*Walks a
few paces*] Now, in the matter of the Bull of
excommunication . . .

CAMPION   [*A trace of bitterness*] Ah, yes. The Bull.
You know, in three years here I never once heard
you express a direct opinion on it. And it's torn
England apart. Driven the Church underground.
Fines, informers, priests tortured. Killed. Tell
me, was excommunicating Elizabeth worth all
that?

ALLEN   It's not for me to judge the mind of a
pope.

CAMPION   At Oxford, I would have called that
evasion.

ALLEN   This isn't Oxford.

CAMPION   They will want *my* opinion on the Bull.
They'll want to know if the Holy Father—and
you—have sent me to help depose the Queen.

ALLEN   [*Sternly*] Then disabuse them of the notion.

The Bull is not a call to overthrow the Queen.
She is sovereign—

CAMPION   [*He's heard it before*] —in all *temporal*
matters.

ALLEN   As long as Elizabeth rules, Catholics are
bound to obey her civil laws.

CAMPION   And to disobey her religious laws. A
neat distinction.

ALLEN   One upon which your life will depend.
[*Awkwardly*] If they capture you, you'll be
questioned. And the question they'll try to hang
you with—the so-called "Bloody Question"
—is this: In the event of an invasion sponsored
by the Pope, would you fight on his side, or the
Queen's?

CAMPION   [*Reflectively*] The question is well named.
And how am I to answer?

ALLEN   [*Heavily*] As truthfully as you can.

[*The moment lingers.*]

CAMPION   Strange to be a missionary in your own
country. [*Cheerfully*] Well—as long as they don't
take me for a Spaniard, eh?

ALLEN   [*Eager to keep the subject light*] I caught two

of the novices this afternoon arguing whether
the Holy Father is financing the King of Spain's
new ships.

CAMPION [*Melodramatically*] Terrible, terrible.
[*Brightly*] In Latin, I trust?

ALLEN For penance, I set them to slops.

CAMPION [*Amused*] That will cure them of politics.

ALLEN There's a lot of bitterness among the new
ones. Their families have suffered, had their
lands confiscated. You were different.

CAMPION [*Smiling*] My family didn't *have* any
land.

ALLEN You gave up more than land.

CAMPION I suppose poping *is* an impediment to a
career in the Anglican church.

ALLEN You'd have been bishop by now instead
of an [*it's a dirty phrase*] exile Catholic priest.

CAMPION [*In pain at the memory; twisting the ring
she gave him*] I regret disappointing the Queen.
She was kind to me.

ALLEN [*Trying to cheer things up*] You were a great
success in Prague, I hear. Professor of Rhetoric.
Praefectus Morum, Praefectus Cubiculi. Di-

rector of the Sodality of the Immaculate Con-
ception. They told me you were in great demand
as a confessor.

CAMPION   I gave light penances.

ALLEN   And playwright to the Emperor!

CAMPION   Perhaps I shall be invited to entertain
the Queen. And her ministers.

ALLEN   [*Suddenly*] It's *bad* in England now. The
Queen would have been content to let the old
priests die off, and the Faith with them. But the
Bull . . . Few priests will die of old age now.
[*Realizing what he's said*] I . . .

CAMPION   [*Kindly*] You're sending me home, to
England.

ALLEN   I burst with joy when the Pope granted
me permission to send you. I should have left
you be in Prague.

CAMPION   [*Forcing the cheer*] The Emperor will
find another playwright. There's Gretser. Or
Fischart. [*Muses*] Though I'm not sure about
Fischart. All those years in Zurich have made
him rather glum.

[*The moment to leave has come. They suddenly
embrace.*]

ALLEN   Good-bye, Edmund. Son. God save you and make you a good priest.

CAMPION   [*Fighting back emotion*] Better he make me slippery, eh?

[*Allen starts to exit.*]

ALLEN   If a stranger calls you "Father", don't answer. We lost Sherwin that way.

[*Campion nods. Allen exits. A shadowy figure (George Eliot) enters, remaining at edge of stage. He watches Campion exit. Lights dim.*]

Scene Eight

A garden outside Richmond Palace, Elizabeth's *residence. Late afternoon. The shadowy figure crosses stage and hands parchment to* Walsingham, *waiting at edge of stage.* Walsingham *reads the report, scowling.*

Elizabeth *enters, upper stage, followed by the* Duke D'Alençon, *younger brother of the French king. He is blindfolded and carries a tennis racquet.* Elizabeth *has a bag of bonbons and is leaving a trail of them for him to find. He squeals with delight as he finds them and pops them in his mouth. She places one on her throne, which he finds, then pulls off his blindfold with a flourish. She sits with him at her feet, feeding him more bonbons.* Walsingham, *watching the scene, scowls.*

Cecil *enters, opposite, lower stage. Looks up at* Elizabeth *and the* Duke, *then crosses to* Walsingham, *who has returned to reading his dispatch.*

CECIL   News?

WALSINGHAM   Yes, news.

CECIL   You are very taciturn today, Francis.

WALSINGHAM   More priests on the way. [*Acidly*] Courtesy of Doctor Allen.

CECIL   [*Sighs*] This supply of continental priests seems inexhaustible.

WALSINGHAM   I told you we should have [*Pointedly*] *dealt* with Allen.

CECIL   [*He's in charge*] No. It would provoke Spain.

WALSINGHAM   [*Shakes the piece of paper in Cecil's face*] *This* is provocation.

CECIL   [*Coolly*] Her Majesty agrees with me. Anyway, your poisoners have tried already three times.

WALSINGHAM   [*Perturbed*] Yes, and the fact that the entire Privy Council is aware of it makes me wonder if Allen was warned.

CECIL   [*Inflamed*] Tread gingerly, Francis. Suspicion in overabundance is not becoming.

WALSINGHAM   I am thinking of Her Majesty's security.

CECIL   I think *only* of Her Majesty's security, Walsingham. From the moment I rise to the moment I lay me down to sleep. And even then my dreams are troubled.

WALSINGHAM   [*Backing down*] You've heard about the omens?

CECIL   Of course I have. You're not the only one who receives reports. Now what about these priests?

WALSINGHAM   This group includes Jesuits.

CECIL   [*Interested*] Oh?

WALSINGHAM   [*Reading from the dispatch*] Ralph
    Emerson, lay brother. Bishop Goldwell of Saint
    Asaph, Dr. Morton, John Pascal, [*Rushing*]
    Gilbert, Crane, Rishton, Kirby, Hart. [*Pauses,
    looks up at Cecil*] Edmund Campion.

CECIL   [*All attention*] Campion?

WALSINGHAM   Edmund Campion, scholar of Ox-
    ford. Who received the Queen's patronage.

CECIL   [*For the record*] And Leicester's. So, they
    are sending him, now. [*Impressed*] The Pope *is*
    earnest. But didn't your last report have him in
    Bohemia, writing tragedies for the Emperor?

WALSINGHAM   Just two months ago. I'll write a
    tragedy for Edmund Campion.

CECIL   [*Can't resist*] I thought Puritans considered
    the theater frivolous. [*Walsingham frowns*] Walk
    with me a while, Francis. [*Looks up*] A fine
    day. I can smell the spring.

WALSINGHAM   [*Looks up and scowls*] I smell rain.

CECIL   [*Glossing*] The Pope has just sent five ships
    to Ireland to aid in the uprising. Five ships,
    under the command of an Englishman. Still the
    Queen will not move against the papists.

WALSINGHAM   Five ships are a trifle. [*With true
    Brit*]*Even* under the command of an Englishman.

CECIL   Exactly. The Queen will remark the Pope's blundering, not bravado. The expedition will be seen for what it is: an ill-begotten alliance with anarchy against decent English order.

WALSINGHAM   Whereas Campion—

CECIL   [*Nodding*] Campion's return will arouse her. [*Rehearsing*] He was her favorite. Now he comes back to England as . . .

WALSINGHAM   An insurrectionist.

CECIL   [*Nodding*] To help depose the Queen. If neither the Papal Bull nor the Pope's ships will convince her that the war has already begun, perhaps Campion's arrival will. [*They both nod, then continue walking*] Indeed, we must be grateful to Pope Gregory for clarifying the Queen's thinking.

WALSINGHAM   [*Matter of factly*] He won't get past Dover.

CECIL   [*Gaily—for him*] I hear that in Dover even the seagulls send you dispatches, Francis. [*The Duke D'Alençon squeals while kissing Elizabeth's ankle. Cecil looks up*] The Duke D'Alençon seems to be enjoying his visit.

WALSINGHAM   He reminds me of a toad.

CECIL   You insult the toad more than the Duke.

WALSINGHAM   She must not marry him.

CECIL   Alliances, Francis, alliances. Tell me, do
you hate him most because he is French, or
because he is Catholic?

WALSINGHAM   I hate him because he is here.

CECIL   She seems fond of him. But she has been
fond of many. Her Majesty will not marry, I
think. [*They start up the stairs*] In the meantime,
cheer yourself. The hopes of English Catholics
hang on *that*.

[*They walk up the stairs to Elizabeth and bow.*]

CECIL   Majesty. [*Rising. To D'Alençon, forcing himself*] Your . . . Grace.

ELIZABETH   Ah. Cecil. [*Still feeding bonbons to
D'Alençon*]

CECIL   There have been certain omens, Ma'am,
much bruited about in the country. The bell of
Westminster rang, apparently on its own. A
woman eighty years of age has given birth to a
monster with eight legs and a tail. [*Elizabeth is
listening now; the Duke grimaces*] Another one
has been reported, covered with hair, resembling
a lion. There's more.

ELIZABETH   [*Quietly; interested*] Go on.

CECIL   There's a report from Wiltshire that a pack
of hounds was seen in the clouds. In Somerset,

armies were sighted moving through the sky at
night.

ELIZABETH   [*Affected*] Anything else?

CECIL   Walsingham has a report of a new infiltra-
tion of continental priests.

ELIZABETH   The ports?

WALSINGHAM   Sealed.

D'ALENÇON   [*With a bad English accent*] England is
a small island. It should not be so hard to keep
people out. [*To Elizabeth*] You are the only
reason to come to England. The weather, the
cuisine . . .

ELIZABETH   [*Amused*] *Arrête*. You are *méchant*.

D'ALENÇON   I am cold. I am hungry. But when
I am with you, my lady, all my appetite are
satisfy! [*He buries himself in Elizabeth's bosom.*]

WALSINGHAM   [*With a look of supreme disgust*] If I
may, Your Majesty.

ELIZABETH   Let me see it. [*She takes the report*]
Who are these [*Mispronouncing it*] Jesu-ites?

WALSINGHAM   Jesuits, Ma'am. A new Spanish
order. They call their superior "General"

CECIL   [*Taking the cue*] That's apt.

WALSINGHAM   There's a name on that list that will
interest Her Majesty.

ELIZABETH   [*Reads, sees the name; her shock is pal-*
    pable] Campion. [*She puts down the report, brushing
    the Duke away*]

CECIL   Who received Her Majesty's patronage.
    [*Lower*] As well as Lord Leicester's.

ELIZABETH   [*Recovering; with eagerness*] So. We knew
    it! He's coming home!

CECIL   As an insurrectionist, Ma'am.

ELIZABETH   [*Convinced*] No. Not Campion.

WALSINGHAM   Be not deceived, Ma'am. Campion
    is not returning to give elegant sermons.

CECIL   You see with what skill these Jesuits recruit,
    Majesty. The most popular man of his day at
    Oxford. [*Pointedly*] The Queen's favorite. Most
    cunning. In truth, there is more to fear in one
    Edmund Campion than in fifty Spanish ships.

ELIZABETH   [*Defensively*] We do not fear Spanish
    ships. But we will not have the Pope and this
    Spanish . . . [*Using the Castilian accent*] Heneral
    sending our former pets against us.

CECIL   Precisely. And there is only one way to
    deal with treason—

ELIZABETH   *We* shall decide if Campion is a traitor,
    Cecil.

CECIL   [*A bit worried*] Surely Her Majesty will not
stoop to treat with a man who has betrayed her
and leagued himself with her enemies?

ELIZABETH   [*Miffed*] You think we are not capable
of disputing with Campion?

CECIL   [*Backing down*] I have seen Her Majesty
joust with many men and unhorse them all.
[*Worried*] Still, he *was* the most celebrated
scholar of his day, and—

ELIZABETH   [*Angry*] So that *is* what you fear. Cecil,
you displease us.

CECIL   [*Retreats a step, bows*] Ma'am.

[*Elizabeth strokes D'Alençon's head and feeds him
another bonbon.*]

ELIZABETH   Walsingham.

WALSINGHAM   Majesty.

ELIZABETH   We wish him brought to us. Unharmed.

WALSINGHAM   He won't get past Dover.

[*A messenger arrives, bows, and hands Walsingham
a report. Walsingham reads it and purses his lips in
such a way that Elizabeth notices.*]

ELIZABETH   What is it?

WALSINGHAM   [*Evasive*] Nothing.

ELIZABETH   [*Piqued*] Nothing? Nothing interests
us so much as nothing. What *is* it, Walsingham?

WALSINGHAM   Campion, Ma'am.

ELIZABETH   Ah. [*Anxious*] You've got him?

WALSINGHAM   [*Uncomfortably*] No. But he is in
England.

ELIZABETH   Oh.

WALSINGHAM   We will have him before long.

ELIZABETH   [*Dropping a bonbon into D'Alençon's
open mouth*] You seem very confident, given
the fact he just slipped through your fingers.

WALSINGHAM   [*Annoyed*] He won't get far.

D'ALENÇON   [*In midcaress*] Shouldn't he be going
to catch his priest? He is not here in the palace, I
think.

ELIZABETH   Go and play your tennis, *mon petit*.

[*Walsingham looks ready to strangle D'Alençon.
He removes himself from Elizabeth's lap. D'Alençon
walks around Walsingham, sizing him up.*]

D'ALENÇON   Black, black, black. All black. Hm.
You look like a priest. You should wear something more gay. [*Looks him up and down with air
of a disapproving tailor, then shakes his head*] *Non*.

[*D'Alençon exits, jauntily.*]

WALSINGHAM [*Bursting*] Your Majesty, I must protest.

ELIZABETH All we are interested in hearing from you, Walsingham, is how you plan to catch Campion.

WALSINGHAM Jesuits are subtle, Ma'am. They come equipped with every continental art.

ELIZABETH Then be artful. Give Campion all your attention. [*Walsingham begins to exit*] Remember, unharmed. [*Walsingham bows and exits*] Cecil.

CECIL Ma'am.

ELIZABETH We are weary of these popish intrigues. It's time for more than fines. [*Cecil nods*] The hangman will serve up a better example of our sincerity.

[*Elizabeth exits, followed by a smiling Cecil.*]

Scene Nine

Stonor, a Catholic house in Oxfordshire. Day. Three wealthy Catholics are waiting, somewhat nervously, for Campion's *arrival.*

FIRST MAN   He's late.

SECOND MAN   [*For the umpteenth time, clearly*] Patience!

FIRST MAN   I don't like it.

[*Suddenly, a coded knocking. The Young Man, Campion's old pupil, enters. The men rush to him.*]

YOUNG MAN   [*Excitedly*] He's here!

[*Campion enters, followed by a beefy bodyguard type. He is "ridiculously" dressed as a rich man, with an ostentatious feather in his hat. The men drop to their knees. Campion bows like a courtier, with a flourish of his hat.*]

FIRST MAN   Father Edmund!

[*Campion looks at the Young Man inquisitively.*]

YOUNG MAN   It's all right. I know all these gentlemen.

CAMPION   [*Abashed*] Forgive me. [*He goes to First Man and embraces him*]

SECOND MAN   Welcome to England, [*With a reproving look at First Man*] *Mister Edmund*.

[*Campion embraces him.*]

THIRD MAN   Aye, welcome!

CAMPION   I bring you all the blessing of the Holy Father in Rome. He bids me tell you this: that he prays all Catholics had such faith as England's. [*To the Young Man*] We'll start as soon as they're all here.

[*The Young Man nods, motions the bodyguard to follow. They go and take their positions, stage right.*]

YOUNG MAN   [*Boastful*] I've known him since Oxford. *Very* close, we are.

FIRST MAN   Faith we have aplenty, Father. Soon that's all we'll have left. The fines will see to that.

ALL   Aye!

CAMPION   [*Cheerfully*] Then we must thank Her Majesty for removing material distractions from our paths. It clears the mind wonderfully for prayer.

[*Dubious glances.*]

SECOND MAN   There was great excitement when we heard you were coming back. The Pope would not have sent Edmund Campion of Oxford back to England just to say a few Masses, eh?

[*More murmuring.*]

FIRST MAN   [*With anticipation*] There's something more afoot, isn't there? Are we to be freed of this tyrant?

CAMPION   The only tyranny I can free you from, friend, is sin.

FIRST MAN   [*Conspiratorially*] You are safe here. You can speak openly.

CAMPION   [*In the same vein, as if about to reveal a great secret*] I may?

FIRST MAN   [*Eagerly*] Yes!

CAMPION   Good, then I will tell you why I've come. [*Pause*] To hear your confessions. And to say Mass.

FIRST MAN   [*Deflated*] I meant only that—

CAMPION   [*Sharply*] That I come to make mischief against the Queen. I do not.

THIRD MAN   [*Stepping in*] Then we welcome you for what you are, Father, and ask your blessing.

CAMPION   [*Touched*] You shall have everything in my power to give.

THIRD MAN   [*With a glance at the others; timidly*] We can't last much longer. Give us permission to attend the Anglican services, blasphemous though they may be. In our hearts we'll still be true to the Catholic Faith.

[*Murmuring.*]

SECOND MAN   I'll plug my ears with wax. Like Odysseus' men!

CAMPION   [*Reluctantly*] I bring guidance from Rome concerning this.

ALL   [*Expectantly*] Yes?

CAMPION   [*Reciting from memory*] "So public an act as is going to the church where profession is made to impugn the truth and to deface, alienate, and bring into hatred Christ's Catholic Church is the"—[*Pauses*]—"highest iniquity that can be committed."

THIRD MAN   That's . . . all?

FIRST MAN   This is the comfort you bring? That we're to be ruined?

CAMPION   When I came into this room a few moments ago, you spoke of the government's tyranny. Then you told me the Queen's church is blasphemous. Now you want the Holy Father's permission to consent to this tyranny and blasphemy because it is too . . . expensive?

FIRST MAN   [*An edge to his voice*] We have families to think of.

CAMPION   Then you will teach your children to be ashamed of their Faith?

FIRST MAN   [*Hotly*] But what good will it do them if we're ruined?

CAMPION   Friend! What good will you do them by depriving them of their greatest inheritance —the Faith of Peter?
    [*Calmly*] Let them impoverish you in this life. They enrich you in the next.

THIRD MAN   Well, I only hope Her Majesty does not enrich me so much in my next life that I no longer have a roof over my head in this one.

[*All laugh, including Campion.*]

FIRST MAN   You must come and explain all this to my lady, Father.

SECOND MAN   Yes, and mine.

CAMPION   [*With humor*] I shall. With some trepidation, I think.

THIRD MAN   [*With resolve*] I'll pay their damn fines. Then that's *all* they'll get from me.

[*Campion nods.*]

FIRST MAN   [*Defiant*] And me.

[*Campion takes them both by the shoulder. A Servant bursts in stage right and tries to push past the Young Man and the bodyguard.*]

YOUNG MAN   Who is it?

SERVANT   [*Urgent, out of breath*] Please, let me in!

YOUNG MAN   On what business?

SERVANT   I seek the Jesuit priest, Father Campion.

YOUNG MAN   There's no priest here.

SERVANT   Please! My master is dying. There's no time.

[*Young Man looks at Campion, who nods at him to open the door. First Man reaches beneath his robe, as if for the hilt of his dagger. Campion shakes his head.*]

YOUNG MAN   But what if it's a trap?

CAMPION   [*Calmly*] What if it's not? [*To the three gentlemen*] Go.

FIRST MAN   We won't leave you.

CAMPION [*With authority*] Go home, to your
families.

[*Reluctantly, the men obey, exiting. Campion motions the Young Man to admit the Servant.*]

SERVANT You are Father Edmund Campion?

CAMPION [*Carefully*] No.

SERVANT I beg you, come with me. My master is
dying. [*Struggling with his emotions*] He was
crushed by his horse two days ago.

CAMPION [*Appearing to see through the man*] Take
me to him.

YOUNG MAN Wait. Who's your master?

SERVANT [*Hesitating*] He is . . . not far from here.
In Reading. Just—

YOUNG MAN I said, *who* is your master?

SERVANT [*Reluctantly*] Miles Frick. Sheriff of
Reading.

YOUNG MAN [*Outraged*] Frick?

[*He lunges at the Servant, pushing him up against
the wall. Campion and the beefy man try to pull
them apart.*]

CAMPION John, stop it!

YOUNG MAN   [*Letting go*] Frick's the one who murdered Father Kearney, the old parish priest here. Probably with the help of this jackal.

[*Campion looks at the Servant.*]

CAMPION·   Is your story true?

[*Servant nods.*]

CAMPION   Then come, quickly. There's no time.

YOUNG MAN   You can't mean it?

CAMPION   This man is not lying.

YOUNG MAN   Lying is his *profession*!

CAMPION   John, listen to me. A man is dying. He's asked for a priest. From what you—you, John—have told me, he may have grievous sins to discharge. Would you deny him?

YOUNG MAN   I'd introduce him to the devil.

CAMPION   You speak as if you've already met him yourself. [*To the Servant*] Come.

[*They exit. Young Man lingers a moment; then he and the bodyguard follow.*]

Scene Ten

Frick's *house. Night. The dying sheriff is on a pallet of straw, attended by women. His rib cage has been crushed. He is in agony and throughout the scene cries out in pain and coughs up blood.*

Campion *and the* Young Man *enter, stage right, led by the* Servant.

SERVANT   Missus.

WIFE   Oh, William!

[*She goes to him. Campion and Young Man are to one side.*]

SERVANT   I've brought him.

WIFE   [*To Campion*] You are Edmund Campion?

[*She moves toward him, as if to embrace him, then remembers herself and holds back.*]

WIFE   [*The respectable housewife*] I am no papist.

[*Frick groans. She stifles a sob.*]

WIFE   [*Plaintively*] Oh, go to him!

[*Campion goes to the bed. The other women move*

82

*away. Campion dips the cloth on Frick's head in
water and wipes his forehead.*]

FRICK   [*With difficulty*] Are . . . you . . .

CAMPION   I am the one you sent for.

FRICK   You came.

CAMPION   You asked for a priest.

FRICK   I was a Catholic. In Queen Mary's time.
Hunted Protestants, then. They changed the
rules. [*Coughs*] You were at Stonor, near Henley.
[*Professional pride*] *Knew* you were there. I could
have got you.

CAMPION   [*Firmly*] I've heard about your skills.
Are you sorry for what you've done?

FRICK   I am sorry I am dying.

CAMPION   Do you ask God's forgiveness?

FRICK   There was a local priest. Father Kearney.
Old man. I caught him saying Mass in a barn.
Know what we did? Threw his Communion
bread to the pigs. [*Laughs, coughs*] Old fool
went running after it. Great sport. So we took
his precious bread, stuck it in pig dung, and
forced it down his throat. He choked to death.
[*Campion is recoiling in horror; Frick, trying to
mask his own horror with a desperate taunt*] Going
to absolve me of *that*, priest?

CAMPION   Why? *Why?*

FRICK   [*In agony*] I have sinned. Help me. I have
    sinned.

CAMPION   Let us pray for Father Kearney. To-
    gether.

[*Frick nods as he gasps.*]

CAMPION   [*Urgently, knowing the end is near*] Pater
    noster . . .

FRICK   [*Barely audible*] Pater noster . . .

CAMPION   *qui es in caelis* . . .

FRICK   *qui* . . . [*Gasps*]

CAMPION   *qui es in caelis* . . .

FRICK   *qui es in caelis* . . .

CAMPION   . . . *sanctificetur nomen tuum, adveniat
    regnum tuum; fiat voluntas tua—*

[*Frick's death rattle starts.*]

CAMPION   [*Produces the tin of oil with an air of great
    urgency*] Can you hear me, Miles? [*Begins
    anointing Frick's forehead*] I absolve you of all
    your sins, in the name of the Father, the Son,
    and the Holy Ghost. [*Frick dies; Campion whis-
    pers, close to his ear*] When you come into the
    kingdom, pray for me.

[*He closes Frick's eyes. Frick's Wife weeps, cradling his head. Campion rises and with the Young Man begins to leave. Suddenly two of the Sheriff's Men enter and block their way.*

   The Young Man bolts but is caught by one of the men.]

CAMPION   [*To Sheriff's First Man*] Let him go. Please. I'm the one you want.

FRICK'S WIFE   [*Standing; with impressive authority*] Stop! [*They freeze*]

SHERIFF'S FIRST MAN   But Missus—

FRICK'S WIFE   [*Fired up*] Take your hands off them. [*They do*] Is this how you honor him in death?

SHERIFF'S FIRST MAN   Missus—the general order. [*Pleading*] Bad enough he asked for a priest. If it's found out—

FRICK'S WIFE   Leave them!

SHERIFF'S FIRST MAN   [*Earnest*] But—they're traitors.

FRICK'S WIFE   [*Walks to Campion*] Are you? [*She takes his hands*] Go now, Father.

[*Campion and the Young Man exit. Lights down. The Sheriff's Men start after them.*]

FRICK'S WIFE   [*Like a schoolmistress*] *Stay* where you are! [*They freeze; she's pleased with herself*] Now we are going to pray. Kneel.

[*She makes them kneel around Frick. She caresses
Frick's head. The men look forlornly out the window
in the direction of the disappearing priest.*]

Scene Eleven

The road outside Reading. Night. Faint light up on Campion *and* Young Man, *walking.*

CAMPION   Let's rest here. [*Sits*] You are silent, John. That is not your natural state.

YOUNG MAN   [*Sullen*] Garrisoned towns take my speech away.

CAMPION   [*Joking*] Then we must arrange to spend more time in them.

YOUNG MAN   [*Can't take it any more*] You come from the bedside of a murderer of priests and you make jests?

CAMPION   I meant only that silence allows us to hear God. As for the other, you are very quick —and very young—to make such judgments on another man.

YOUNG MAN   Oh, I see. I'm to pity him. [*Angry*] Well, I *knew* Father Kearney. He baptized me. And he was lucky to have died as he did. And I've known others [*Can hardly bring himself to mention the name*] Miles Frick brought to the Queen's justice! Have you ever seen a man hanged, cut down alive, and his guts drawn out

and burnt in front of him? They scream and beg
for death, only not so comfortably as Master
Miles Frick back there, surrounded by family
and the comfort of a priest! No, I don't forgive
so easily.

CAMPION   [*He explodes*] You? *You* don't forgive
so easily? Who are *you* to send a man to hell?
Dust! Nothing! We must be grateful that Miles
Frick is beyond *your* forgiveness. As for me, I
pray that when my time comes I will make half
as good a death as he.

YOUNG MAN   I meant only—

CAMPION   [*Gently*] You meant only that you loved
Father Kearney. Love God first, John. [*Taking
him by both shoulders*] Do that, and you will love
all men well enough.
     [*Looks up at the sky*] It's dark. [*To himself*] Not
much time left.
     John, I'm going to write something. I want
you to deliver it to London for me, have it
dated, witnessed, and sealed. It is only to be
opened—this is essential John—*only* to be
opened and made public in the event of my
capture. Understood? [*The Young Man nods*]
Good lad.

     [*Campion sits, removes a parchment and quill pen
     from his pack, and begins to write.*]

CAMPION   To Her Majesty, Elizabeth, Queen of

England, and the Right Honorable Lords of Her Majesty's Privy Council—

Whereas I have come out of Germany and Boemeland, being sent by my superiors, and adventured myself into this noble realm, my dear country, for the glory of God and benefit of souls, I thought it like enough that, in this busy, watchful, and suspicious world, I should sooner or later be intercepted and stopped in my course.

I supposed it needful to put this writing in readiness, desiring your lordships to give it your reading, for to know my cause.

[*Stands, starts to speak directly to the audience*]

I am loth to speak anything that might sound like an insolent brag or challenge, especially being now as a dead man to this world. But I do most humbly ask for the privilege of debate with you, so as to vouch for the majesty of Jesus, my King, assuring you that the better furnished you come, the more welcome you will be.

We of the Society of Jesus have made a league—cheerfully to carry the cross you have laid on us and never to despair your recovery, while we have a man left to enjoy your Tyburn, or to be racked with your torments, or consumed by your prisons.

The expense is reckoned; the enterprise is be-

gun. So the Faith was planted. So it must be restored.

[*Sudden, violent sounds offstage, the arrival of many
men. The Young Man flees. Campion starts to exit
offstage, then, seeing his escape cut off, hides under
the bench, a "priest-hole" in a large house.*]

Scene Twelve

A Catholic house in the country. Night. Several men with truncheons and torches enter.

HEAD SEARCHER   You—to the north wing.

FIRST SEARCHER   I've searched it.

HEAD SEARCHER   [*Impatiently*] Then search it *again*! [*To the others*] Light fires in all the chimneys; see if they've been blocked. [*Calling after them*] And don't forget the roof!

[*They fan out, some going up the stairs, others disappearing backstage, shouting and banging the walls with their truncheons. The Searchers tap the walls, pull some planking loose. One is quite near Campion, under the bench.*]

SECOND SEARCHER   They're like ferrets, these priests.

HEAD SEARCHER   Ferrets need to eat and drink, sooner or later. Harder, damn you! Afraid of scratching the wainscotting? [*The man obeys, banging harder*]

SECOND SEARCHER   There's one sure way of knowing.

HEAD SEARCHER   [*Impatient*] Well?

SECOND SEARCHER   [*Enjoying himself*] Burn it down.
See if any maggots crawl out.

HEAD SEARCHER   It would be less trouble. Oh, this
is useless. [*To the men still on the scaffolding*] You
up there! Enough.

[*They exit.*]

Scene Thirteen

Same house. Some moments after the searchers have left, Campion *unwedges himself from his hiding space. It is painful; his limbs are cramped, and he pulls himself away, wincing.*

The Young Man *rushes in, looking about nervously. He sees* Campion *and goes to him.*

YOUNG MAN   Father! [*Starts rubbing Campion's limbs*]

CAMPION   [*Shaking*] I'm all right.

YOUNG MAN   I was in the woods.

CAMPION   How long were they here? I lost track.

YOUNG MAN   Two days. [*Campion is trying to wake up his legs, which have fallen asleep*] They had cannon trained on the front.

CAMPION   Cannon? Honestly. Did they think the *house* would try to escape?

YOUNG MAN   They don't know what they think. They're tearing apart every Catholic house in England, trying to find the author of "Campion's Brag".

CAMPION   [*With an air of intellectual disappointment*]
I wish they wouldn't call it that. I only asked
for a hearing before the Privy Council. John, I
do wish you hadn't shown it to anyone.

YOUNG MAN   I only showed it to Sir Thomas. I
didn't know he'd made a copy—

CAMPION   [*Reassuringly*] I know. I know.

YOUNG MAN   Maybe the Queen has decided to
give you one.

CAMPION   [*Laughs*] If these are her messengers, I
don't think debate is what she has in mind.
[*A moment passes*] John—

YOUNG MAN   What is it, Father?

CAMPION   [*Realizing it for the first time*] I'm . . .
frightened. [*It hangs there; he rises stiffly, trying to
summon strength*] No time to waste, now.

YOUNG MAN   [*Trying to cheer him*] They haven't
found you yet.

CAMPION   They will. They have too many eyes
and too many tongues.
   They *have* to find me, don't you see? They've
spread the word I'm here to make rebellion.
Say "Jesuit" and they see Spanish ships. [*Ad-
miring their shrewdness*] Oh, yes. The threat of
war with Spain serves them very well. Don't
you see? Cecil and Walsingham are using it to
clean house.

[*Suddenly remembering himself*] John, I must not speak to you of these things. [*Directly*] I have *not* spoken to you of these things. Understood?

[*Young Man nods.*]

CAMPION   Now I want you to go to Dame Cecily at Stonor. Tell her I have need of her attic for a month or so.

YOUNG MAN   [*Suspicious*] Her attic?

CAMPION   The space must be large enough to contain a small printing press.

YOUNG MAN   A printing press? Why?

CAMPION   For the making of a book.

YOUNG MAN   Oh, Father, not *another* declaration! You'll provoke them!

CAMPION   [*Pointed toward the departed searchers*] They are already "provoked", John.
   But they are also afraid. I must support with solid argument what I put forth in my letter to the Privy Council. [*The scholar, talking to himself*] It must be in Latin, scrupulously accurate, all scriptural references annotated and checked. If I misplace a single syllable, they'll hang me with it.

YOUNG MAN   It's madness.

CAMPION   No. Don't you see? It's our best weap-
    on. They fear the truth more than they fear me.
    They can't hang a book.

YOUNG MAN   They can burn books. And hang
    those who write them.

CAMPION   *Ignem veni mittere in terram*, John. "I am
    come to send fire on the earth." Now go!

[*The Young Man runs out.*]

Scene Fourteen

Campion *turns to the audience and "reads" his book in a sharp voice. As he does,* Elizabeth *enters, upper stage left, holding the book and reading it with mounting anger.*

CAMPION "*Decem Rationes*—Ten Reasons, for the confidence with which Edmund Campion offered his adversaries to dispute on behalf of the Faith, set before the famous men of the Universities.

"Listen, Elizabeth, most powerful Queen, I tell thee: One and the same heaven cannot hold Calvin and all the English princes and saints I have named. With *these* Princes of the Church associate thyself, and so make thee worthy of thy ancestors and worthy of thy genius.

"To this effect only do I labor about thy person, and will labor, whatever shall become of me. Hail the Good Cross!"

[*He turns to face Elizabeth; she glares at him*]

"There will come the day that will show thee clearly which have loved thee best, the Society of Jesus or the offspring of Luther."

[*Elizabeth closes the book. Campion exits. She descends the staircase.*]

97

Scene Fifteen

Richmond Palace. Day. Cecil, Walsingham, Leicester, *and the* Duke D'Alençon *enter at various points.*

CECIL   The deans are already at work on a refutation, Majesty. The task has been given to Doctor Charke.

ELIZABETH   Charke? [*Disdainful*] We shall see what good comes of that. [*She turns on Walsingham*] In the meantime, we do not understand how Campion managed to distribute this—this—book on commencement day at Oxford. [*The Duke sniggers; Cecil avoids eye contact*] Walsingham!

WALSINGHAM   Oxford is sealed, Ma'am. Nothing moves, in or out of it, without my knowledge.

ELIZABETH   Except, apparently, Jesuit priests dispensing books by the cartload! Bah! One morning we shall awake to the Spanish fleet anchored in our moat, and you will say, "Nothing comes up the Thames without my knowing it"!

CECIL   [*Peacemaking*] Sir Francis is doing everything he can. The incident clearly shows the

extent of Campion's malice against you. And
how dangerous he is.

D'ALENÇON   Walsingham, I think you have a
problem with this priest.

WALSINGHAM   Majesty, I protest!

[*Elizabeth rebukes the Duke with a glance. He
retreats behind his powderpuff.*]

LEICESTER   [*Whispering*] Is it prudent, Ma'am, that
his grace should attend our conference on this
matter?

ELIZABETH   His mind is on other things.

[*D'Alençon is powdering his face at the mirror.*]

LEICESTER   [*Businesslike*] Why doesn't Her Majesty
make him the proposition we discussed?

CECIL   [*Concerned*] What "proposition"?

LEICESTER   Canterbury. He was headed there, anyway, before he poped. [*Cajoling*] I'm sure he
could be persuaded. He would be a sensational
acquisition.

[*Elizabeth appears to consider this for a moment, but
then turns abruptly to Walsingham.*]

ELIZABETH   Why can't you find him, Walsingham
—despite the [*Sarcastic*] excellence of your secret
service?

WALSINGHAM   He moves about with no set pattern, in a variety of disguises. [*In D'Alençon's direction*] For all we know, he could be disguised as a French duke. We don't know what he looks like.

ELIZABETH   [*Hurls the book at him*] *We* know what he looks like! We have spent *hours* with him! Days!

WALSINGHAM   [*Fiercely*] Over ten years ago!

[*She and Walsingham face off, ready to go for each other's throats. Francis Walsingham was the only man Elizabeth was said to fear.*]

LEICESTER   I know a man. [*He's playing for effect*]

ELIZABETH   [*Impatiently*] Well?

LEICESTER   His name is Eliot. He sent me some letters from jail, offering information about his former employers—Catholics. They'd been harboring priests. The information was reliable.

ELIZABETH   Why was he in jail?

LEICESTER   [*Hesitantly*] Rape, Ma'am

ELIZABETH   Ah.

LEICESTER   [*As an afterthought*] And homicide.

ELIZABETH   What interesting people you know, Robin. We must have him to palace.

LEICESTER   [*Getting back at Walsingham*] At least *he* knows what Campion looks like. Of course, he does not have the skills of Sir Francis' men.

D'ALENÇON   My grandmother have more talent than his men. And she have been dead for twenty years.

ELIZABETH   [*French*] *Si-lence!*

LEICESTER   He has been responsible for the capture of over a dozen priests.

ELIZABETH   Then have this [*Acidly*] gentleman find Campion. We shall be in his debt.

LEICESTER   Oh, undoubtedly.

[*Leicester bows, and exits.*]

ELIZABETH   [*Musing*] To catch a priest with a murderer. . . . The proposition lacks elegance. [*Gravely*] Do what you must.

[*All exit. Walsingham picks up the book as he goes and slaps it against his other hand angrily. Lights down.*]

Scene Sixteen

Lyford Grange, a country house. Late afternoon.
Campion is center, wearing a chasuble. A semicircle of
men and women are in front of him, hearing Mass in an
attitude of devotion. The Young Man *is at stage right,*
admitting latecomers in pantomime. First Man *whispers*
the password and is let in. Second Man *whispers the*
password and is let in. George Eliot *appears, whispers*
the password. The Young Man *hesitates, but* Eliot
glides by him. There is something slightly off about
Eliot. *He takes his place at the edge of the congregation.*

Campion elevates the Host. As he lowers it, he sees
Eliot. *They connect.* Campion *recognizes his betrayer;*
Eliot *his quarry.* Eliot *is about to run to get the sheriff*
and the searchers but for a second is frozen to the spot,
recognizing in that split moment the evil he is about to
do. The shadow passes, and he slinks away. Campion's
eyes follow him for several instants, then he genuflects
and completing the rite of consecration of the Host,
aware that the searchers are coming.

Three heavy knocks on a door. Lights down.

End Act One

ACT TWO

Scene One

A dungeon beneath the Tower of London; and Cecil's *chambers. Night or day. Lights up.* Campion *is wedged beneath the bench, inside the "Little Ease", the cruelly small cells where new prisoners were kept on their arrival at the Tower.*

On upper stage, left, Cecil *is standing at his writing desk, a servant behind him.* Leicester *enters, lower stage, and climbs staircase.*

LEICESTER   What are you going to do with him?

CECIL   [*Mildly*] Examine him.

LEICESTER   Rack him, you mean.

CECIL   That's up to him.

LEICESTER   He's been in the Little Ease four days now. You may not have to. [*Walks a few steps; looks into distance, as if through a window*] This has to be handled carefully, Cecil.

CECIL   [*Going about his paperwork*] I have no desire to give Rome another martyr. But the man's a traitor.

LEICESTER   Oh, for God's sake, Cecil, the man's no more an agent of Spain than I am.

CECIL   [*Appearing to consider the possibility*] Walsingham disagrees with you.

LEICESTER   Walsingham sees Spaniards in his piss pot.

CECIL   [*Minatory*] He would not enjoy hearing you say that. [*Back to business*] Anyway, I have . testimony that Campion helped to convey thirty thousand pounds to the Irish rebels.

LEICESTER   [*Dubious*] Testimony? From whom?

CECIL   Meanwhile, he will be questioned.

LEICESTER   You won't get anything from him about that.

CECIL   We shall see.

LEICESTER   [*Trying to find a way*] Why not just leave him where he is for a while? A year or two in the Tower is bound to cool his Catholic fire.

CECIL   [*Out of patience*] You can't deal with Catholics that way. They *enjoy* suffering. Makes them feel holy.

LEICESTER   There, from your own mouth. You know he has no political motives. It's religion.

CECIL   Nonetheless, he presents potential political problems.

LEICESTER   You know how she feels about torture.

CECIL   [*Cutting him off*] If you haven't the stomach for affairs of state, Leicester, I suggest you go back to your bears.

[*Leicester draws himself up; Cecil's stare stops him. Leicester storms out. Cecil signs the warrant of torture and hands it to the servant. Lights dim, upper stage.*]

Scene Two

The dungeons beneath the White Tower. Night or day. The servant descends stairs. Two jailers appear, with Norton, *the* Queen's *"commissioner". The servant hands the warrant to* Norton, *who motions the other men to drag* Campion *from the Little Ease.*

The "rack" is against the wall, backstage: a horizontal bar hung from a chain looped over a hook suspended by ropes attached to a pulley.

They shackle Campion *to the bar and hoist on the rope, lifting him a few inches into the air.*

Norton *interrogates him in silence. Lights down.*

Scene Three

Various townspeople enter left and right. A guard takes his position by the stairs.

OLD WOMAN Have'e heard?

FIRST MAN Wha'bout?

OLD WOMAN The Jesuit. Campion. He's turned Protestant.

FIRST MAN Campion? Naah!

OLD WOMAN Aye. And accepted a bishop's seat.

FIRST MAN [*Impressed*] No!

SECOND MAN That's right. And he's to make a public statement at Saint Paul's Cross.

OLD WOMAN He's going to burn his "Ten Reasons".

SECOND MAN Better his pamphlet than him, eh? [*Laughter*] They've arrested many on the information he's given them.

OLD WOMAN Purchased his safety by betraying his friends. [*Spits*]

109

SECOND MAN   Ah, to the devil with them. They deserve each other. Let them all hang.

FIRST MAN   Bishop he's to be? Well, he *has* conformed.

[*Third Man, well dressed, approaches the Guard. We recognize him as one of those who welcomed Campion on his return to England. He has an air of gentlemanly authority.*]

THIRD MAN   The streets are full of gossip about this Campion fellow, guard.

GUARD   Oh, yes, sir. Very celebrated guest, you might say.

THIRD MAN   No visitors, I don't suppose.

[*Guard laughs. Man produces a purse and takes out a coin.*]

THIRD MAN   This gossip, one doesn't know what to believe. But I should think a man of your station would have *reliable* news.

[*The Guard slips the coin into his tunic.*]

GUARD   [*Furtively*] Well, I did hear . . .

THIRD MAN   Yes?

YEOMAN   . . . that the rackmaster has made good on his promise to stretch him four inches.

[*The Guard laughs uproariously. The Third Man exits with horror and disgust.*]

Scene Four

Cecil's *chambers. Day.* Cecil *at his desk.* Norton *goes up the stairs to him.*

CECIL   [*Looks up*] Well?

NORTON   [*Proudly*] I have the Jesuit's confession, my lord. It took a good bit of stretching to get it from him.

CECIL   [*Going back to his papers*] Read it to me.

NORTON   [*Reading*] On October 14 he did visit Henry Pierpont and his brother Jervis and say Masses. He did confess both the Pierponts every week.

On November 2 he confessed Henry Sacheverell and said one Mass.

November 23 he confessed the Lady Ffuljames . . . [*Cecil ceases writing but does not look up*] . . . and tarried there, saying *three* Masses.

On Christmas, he did—

CECIL   [*Exploding*] Masses? Confessions? [*Exploding*] Is this all? Is this *all* you got from him?

NORTON   [*Taken aback*] There's more, my Lord. [*Reads again, fumbling, nervous*] On twelfth night he stayed with the Vavasours and there did say two Masses each day, confessing numerous members of the household, including—

CECIL   Enough. [*Rubs his forehead*]

NORTON   [*Certain the best is yet to come*] But these names . . . many of them are Protestant.

CECIL   [*Temper rising*] He was ministering to their *servants*. [*Sighs*] He told you nothing more?

NORTON   [*Shakes his head in sincerity*] Oh, believe me, my lord. I would be surprised if he had kept anything back. It was a most rigorous session.

CECIL   [*Very pointedly*] He is a seditionist, Norton. Do you understand?

NORTON   [*Nodding*] I understand, my lord.

[*Norton walks back down the staircase. Cecil goes on writing. Lights dim.*]

Scene Five

Tower dungeons. Norton directs the torturers to drag Campion from his "cell" to the rack. They shackle him to it and hoist him up, this time with greater violence. Campion emits a single, long piercing scream. Lights down.

Scene Six

Cecil's *chambers. Day.* Cecil *writing. The jailers bring* Campion *up the stairs, chained. His hands are crippled from the torture; he holds them at waist level, as if cradling a baby. He limps.*

CECIL   [*Without looking up*] Ah, Mr. Campion. I trust you are enjoying your stay with us. [*He sees Campion's condition and is embarrassed, but hides it*] There are some questions, some questions you have not answered.

CAMPION   [*Firmly*] What are you going to do to the people whose names I gave you under torture?

CECIL   They are of no consequence to our present discussion.

CAMPION   [*Fiery*] They are of great consequence to me!

CECIL   [*Amused*] You are in no position to make demands. But no harm . . . need come to them.

CAMPION   Will you swear to that?

CECIL   [*Affronted*] I do not swear oaths to prisoners.

CAMPION   Then I have nothing further to say.

CECIL   Your obstinacy leaves me little choice—

CAMPION   But to "question" me again? Do so.

CECIL   [*Matter of fact*] You will confess. Everyone does, you know.

CAMPION   [*As if he might*] To what?

CECIL   [*Picks up the confession*] That you came into England under instructions of the false Bishop of Rome and in league with the King of Spain to make rebellion against our sovereign Queen, Elizabeth.

CAMPION   [*Appearing to consider it*] You want me to confess to that?

CECIL   Your signature on the document. That is all.

CAMPION   [*Stepping forward toward the desk, where the confession lies; he seems ready to sign*] I would have to swear, upon my oath, that this confession were true, wouldn't I?

CECIL   [*Warily*] A mere formality . . .

CAMPION   [*An ironic laugh*] Ah, a "formality". Lying before God.

CECIL   It's not God you should be concerning yourself with at the moment, Campion.

CAMPION   [*Gently*] However inhospitable the Tower
    may be, my lord, it is but a poor resemblance of
    where I should spend eternity if I were to swear,
    upon my oath, to [*Distastefully*] that.

CECIL   [*Down to business*] The evidence against
    you is overwhelming.

CAMPION   [*Trying to find some area of decency within
    him*] Do *you* believe that, my lord?

CECIL   [*Dodging it*] And you will be found guilty
    of treason. Be sure of it.
        You once found favor with the Queen. You
    may yet again. [*Offering him the confession*] It's
    up to you.

CAMPION   I pray that I might.

CECIL   [*Darkly*] It will take more than prayer.

    [*Cecil signals for the guards. They remove Campion
    and take him back down the stairs.*]

Scene Seven

Campion's *cell in the Tower. The guards throw* Campion *roughly to the ground. His prayer comes out in gasps.*

CAMPION Lord, forgive me. I meant to betray none. . . . I tried. . . . Grant that my suffering might mitigate theirs, and in thy tender mercy, keep them— [*Shrieks in pain*] Oh, God, God! Let some better man endure this. You have so many others stronger than I. Better men. I cannot . . .

[*Jailer has come onstage and looked at Campion writhing with a flicker of sympathy. He dips a ladle into a water bucket, raises Campion's head, and gives him a drink.*]

CAMPION Bless you.

JAILER [*Not unkindly*] Don't go blessing me. It would only be trouble for me.

CAMPION You are kind. [*Sinks back*] God *is* with us.

JAILER [*Grunts*] God? Here? D'you know where you are, man? The Salt Tower. God isn't here,

I tell you. [*Looks about, with no sense of his own wit*] It's not 'is sort of place.

CAMPION   Yes. He is. [*Quoting*] "I was thirsty, and ye bade me drink."

JAILER   [*Miffed*] That was me, Jack Delahays, wot brought you water, not Jaysus.

[*He gives Campion another sip, gets him to his feet, and sits him on a stool.*]

Scene Eight

Saint John's Chapel, the Tower. Day. Three Anglican Deans, *including* Charke, *enter. During the disputation, they remain on their feet, circling about* Campion.

CAMPION   Dean already, Doctor Charke? Congratulations.

CHARKE   [*Ignoring it*] We are outraged, Mr. Campion, to find, among the many lies, blasphemies, and deceptions in your "Ten Reasons" [*Holds up the book*] an accusation of [*Reading from it*] "uncommon cruelty" against Her Majesty's most merciful government, as well as the contemptible allegation that her Anglican bishops have offered [*Again, reading*] "torture instead of conference".

CAMPION   [*Wryly, holding up his hands*] Here's *my* evidence.

CHARKE   [*Sharply*] You will answer direct questions. This is not Oxford.

CAMPION   [*Looks about*] I would not have mistaken this place for Oxford.

CHARKE You have confessed to great crimes, among them that you have said Masses.

CAMPION Yes, I am guilty of that. But now, I have a different notion of "confession"—

SECOND DEAN You have used devious devices, to effect, but no one here is fooled.

CAMPION [*Nodding*] Oh, I can see that.

THIRD DEAN We have heard you cite Luther, and yet you have failed to find the citation.

CAMPION [*He's been through this already*] Because you gave me the expurgated Wittenberg edition, and not the unexpurgated Jena—

CHARKE [*Pouncing*] You misquoted Tertullian!

CAMPION [*Calmly*] I was brought here in the middle of the night. You didn't give me any time for preparation.

SECOND DEAN [*Contemptuously*] Even your Greek was ungrammatical.

CAMPION [*Sincerely*] True enough. It was never very good, really. They say I speak it with a Bohemian accent.

CHARKE Why do you continue to uphold the real presence in the Mass, despite the plain fact that doctrine clearly denies the bodily presence of Christ?!

CAMPION   [*Firmly*] *Your* doctrine. Why must you
   confine him to the properties of a natural body?
   Heaven is his palace. You would make it his
   prison.

SECOND DEAN   You are an unnatural man to your
   country, degenerate from an Englishman, apostate in religion, fugitive from the realm, and
   disloyal to your prince.

THIRD DEAN   Returned to plant secretly the blasphemous Mass!

CAMPION   [*Slowly*] Is it unnatural to love your
   fellow countrymen? Or apostate to be of the
   same Faith as Augustine and Edward Confessor
   and Thomas à Becket? They are the fugitives of
   which you speak, for you have driven them
   from the hearts of Englishmen. To be fugitive
   with them is no dishonor, but great glory.
      I am loyal to my Queen, and pray for her with
   all my remaining strength.
      And touching the Mass, which you now hold
   "blasphemous", let me ask: How is it that
   this [*Spits it out*] *insight* has remained hidden
   from the world for fifteen centuries and now
   stands, suddenly revealed, to such a [*A sad smile,
   shake of his head*] *select* group of Englishmen?

CHARKE   Hold your tongue, Jesuit. You're a prisoner here.

CAMPION   [*Disappointed at the shabbiness of their*

arguments] Forgive me. I had forgotten my station.

CHARKE   We have proven your lack of scholarship. What say you?

CAMPION   [*Wearily*] That I am the Queen's prisoner, Doctor Charke, not yours.

CHARKE   Remove him.

[*The guards take him back to his cell, lower stage. Deans exit. Lights down.*]

Scene Nine

Cecil's *chambers. Day.* Leicester *enters, upper stage; goes to* Cecil, *at his desk.* Cecil's *servant stands to one side.*

LEICESTER   You've seen the report of the debate?

CECIL   [*Heavily*] I have.

LEICESTER   Well?

CECIL   [*As if reciting an unpleasant exercise in grammar*] Our learned church doctors have ably demonstrated the Jesuit's blasphemy, sham scholarship, and malicious intent.

LEICESTER   [*Dubious*] A possibly . . . unique interpretation.

CECIL   [*Authoritatively*] Mine, nonetheless.

LEICESTER   [*Enjoying Cecil's discomfiture*] Do you know what the ballad mongers are saying?

CECIL   [*Trying to sustain the façade with difficulty*] I have no interest in street rabble.

LEICESTER   Oh, this *will* interest you.

[*A Woman enters and crosses lower stage.*]

WOMAN   [*Singing*]

123

"A Jesuit, a Jesuite? Wherefore I you pray?
Because he doth teach you the only right
way?
He professeth the same by learning to prove
And shall we from learning to rack him
remove.

"His reasons were ready, his grounds were
most sure,
The enemy cannot his force long endure,
Campion in camping on spiritual field
In God's cause his life is ready to yield.

"Our preachers have preached in pastime
and pleasure,
And now they be hated far passing all
measure;
Their wives and their wealth have made
them so mute,
They cannot nor dare not with Campion
dispute."

[*She exits.*]

CECIL   Doggerel. [*Leicester stares him down*] But
dangerous doggerel, I grant. It's time to con-
clude this business.

LEICESTER   Cecil— [*Cecil glares at him as if to say,
"Don't start"*] There must be some way.

CECIL   There is *indeed* a way.

LEICESTER   Exile him.

CECIL   We do not exile traitors. Listen to me, Leicester, this is *your* mess. *You* found him; *you* patronized him—

LEICESTER   [*Showing his guilt*] And, damn it, *I* saw to his capture.

CECIL   [*Sarcastically*] Yes. Under the circumstances, the least you owed the Queen. And yet to judge from your incessant—and exceedingly tiresome —interventions on behalf of the traitor, your conscience seems to be ailing. You should have it looked at, Leicester. Have it bled.

LEICESTER   [*Flaring*] Careful.

CECIL   [*Very cool, almost amused*] Are *you* threatening me, my lord?

LEICESTER   [*Backing down*] The Queen still has feelings for him.

CECIL   [*He's thought this through*] She won't once she learns the real reason he returned.

LEICESTER   Oh, he's been racked twice, for God's sake! Stretched *four inches*. Nearly killed. And what have you got?

CECIL   [*Mildly*] He has a stern constitution.

LEICESTER   [*Utter perplexity*] It's not that. I don't know what it is. But it's not that.

CECIL   [*Taking another warrant of torture and signing it, handing it to his servant*] Then we must find out what *it* is.

[*The servant takes the warrant and exits. Leicester storms off. Cecil returns to his paperwork.*]

Scene Ten

The Tower, Campion's *cell. Night.* Leicester *enters. Goes to where* Campion *is lying, asleep.*

LEICESTER [*Horrified*] Christ. [*Leans down*] Edmund. Edmund!

CAMPION [*Peering up*] My . . . lord? [*Struggles to get up to his feet. Leicester, embarrassed, helps him onto the bench.*] My lord!

LEICESTER [*Recovered*] Look at you.

[*Campion looks at his robe.*]

CAMPION [*Bemused*] Yes, look at me. Not very suitable attire for an audience with the Master of the Horse. Do you remember the purse of gold you gave me that day at Oxford?

LEICESTER I remember a young scholar with a future.

CAMPION [*Looking about his cell*] Well, here's the future.

LEICESTER [*Pointedly; this is all Campion's fault*] Not very bright, is it?

CAMPION   It's night. [*No windows in the cell*] Or is it?

LEICESTER   Listen to me, Edmund. You still have a future.

CAMPION   I am every bit as glad to hear it now as I was when you told me that fifteen years ago.

LEICESTER   [*Thinks he's getting through*] Good. Good! You can be out of here this evening. [*Campion looks at him hopefully*] There's someone come to see you.

[*Elizabeth enters, covered with a cape.*]

CAMPION   *Majesty!*

[*Leicester bows. Campion clumsily tries to rise and bow, wincing with pain.*]

ELIZABETH   [*Surprised*] You are hurt, Mr. Campion. [*Turns on Leicester*] I gave instructions that he was to be treated well!

LEICESTER   My lord Cecil—

ELIZABETH   [*Furiously*] Has disobeyed me! Leave us, Leicester.

[*Leicester bows and withdraws.*]

ELIZABETH   [*Awkwardly*] We are sorry to find you this way, Mr. Campion. We do not approve of torture.

CAMPION   I'm not sure that the royal attitude has been made sufficiently clear to Her Majesty's servants. [*Elizabeth smiles in spite of herself*] Still, I am honored to see my Queen again, despite the circumstances.

ELIZABETH   You speak like a courtier. You call me "Queen"? Am I still your Queen?

CAMPION   You are.

ELIZABETH   [*Unconvinced*] We are pleased to hear it. And surprised.

CAMPION   I have always acknowledged your sovereignty, Ma'am.

ELIZABETH   Oh, yes, we do not dispute *that*. You have always acknowledged our sovereignty. You acknowledged it from Ireland, from that seminary on the continent, from Prague, and from Rome. If all my subjects were as loyal as you, I should have no one to rule.

CAMP ION   [*Laughs*] Well, here I am. Back in . . . [*With bite*] merry England. Your loyal subject. [*Serious*] Who has always recognized you as his lawful and beloved Queen . . . in all temporal matters.

ELIZABETH   [*A bit sarcastic*] Oh, of course. All *temporal* matters. Taxes, lighting bonfires on our birthday, drinking to our health, petitioning our courts for assorted ill-deserved privileges. We are very grateful.

CAMPION   Is it not enough for Her Majesty that her Catholic subjects would die for her? Or does she require more?

ELIZABETH   [*A little hot*] We require only that Englishmen live by the law.

CAMPION   What kind of justice jails a man for obeying God's law?

ELIZABETH   *We* determine God's law.

CAMPION   No.

ELIZABETH   [*Not used to hearing the word*] "No"? [*Furious*] "No"?!

CAMPION   [*Desperate*] You are Queen of England, my Queen, mistress of every mortal part of Edmund Campion. But not his soul. That belongs to God.

ELIZABETH   To God, or the false Bishop of Rome?

CAMPION   [*Angrily*] I am a Catholic man, Lady!
    [*Calmly, as if pointing out a simple technicality*] Really, it's a simple distinction between two concepts, the *potestas ordinata* of the secular ruler, and the *potestas inordinata* of the spiritual rul—

ELIZABETH [*Impatient*] I grasp the distinction, thank you.

CAMPION Yes. Yes, of course you do. [*Teasing*] We had the same tutor, didn't we?

ELIZABETH [*Brightening*] Doctor Ascham! Did he ever challenge you to a footrace?

CAMPION He was a walking man by the time he got to me. [*Elizabeth puffs up, miffed about the reference to her age; he beats a retreat*] No doubt Her Majesty had worn him out prematurely with her swiftness of foot and mind.

ELIZABETH [*Relaxing*] Ah. We held him very dear. He gambled.

CAMPION Oh, I know.

ELIZABETH Always in debt. We wanted to make him prebendary at York, but [*Sighs*] for that. At least we were able to take care of his debts.

CAMPION Did he teach you archery?

ELIZABETH Yes! But we prefer the crossbow to the long bow.

CAMPION One day when I came to preach to Her Majesty's court at Rycote, she killed five harts.

ELIZABETH Six.

CAMPION Then Doctor Ascham taught you very well.

ELIZABETH   We recognized his influence in you that day we heard you speak at Oxford.

CAMPION   [*Teasing*] Could it be because I likened Her Majesty to the goddess Diana?

ELIZABETH   [*Girlishly*] Well . . . in fact we do recall it.

CAMPION   Her Majesty is called by many names. Pandora, Gloriana, Cynthia, Belphoebe . . .

ELIZABETH   [*Prompting*] Astraea.

CAMPION   I was getting to that.

[*They laugh.*]

ELIZABETH   We are not beautiful. [*Campion about to protest*] We *were* beautiful. When we were younger. [*She sits down beside him*] But it is more pleasant to be called by those names than Rebekkah, whore of Babylon, which I am called by those of the Romish persuasion. Did Doctor Ascham teach you ingratitude as well as Greek?

CAMPION   He taught me to look for the truth.

ELIZABETH   [*Bitterly*] And you found the truth in Rome?

CAMPION   It was not Doctor Ascham who chased me to Rome but Her Majesty's theologians.

ELIZABETH   We do not care for theologians.

CAMPION   [*Teasing*] Is that why she submits to their sermons only during Lent?

ELIZABETH   They make ropes of sand and sea slime, leading nowhere.

CAMPION   Well, somewhere.

ELIZABETH   [*Suddenly*] Oh, Edmund! That is why we wanted *you* for Canterbury!

CAMPION   [*Struggling with his emotions*] If only I could have, my Lady. I so . . . wanted it.

[*Elizabeth takes his hands. He winces.*]

ELIZABETH   Your hands. Sweet, beautiful hands that once caressed the air as you preached to us at Rycote. [*She leans down and kisses each hand*] Sweet hands, so foully used.

[*They remain like this for some moments, looking at each other, almost as if they might collapse into each other's arms. Elizabeth gently gives him back his hands, as if she were making him a gift of them.*]

ELIZABETH   [*Changing the subject, fighting back tears*] We hear you were a great success in Prague. Playwright to the Emperor. [*Campion seems to shrug; Elizabeth can't bear to look at him; walks some paces away, looking away*] Is his court very gay?

CAMPION   [*Absently*] Oh, yes, very.

ELIZABETH   We hear that it is. Was it more . . .
amusing than our own?

CAMPION   In truth [*About to rave; then checks himself*]
there was none there to match Her Majesty's
conversation. But it was pleasant enough at
times to make me forget that I missed England.
[*Looks down at his mangled hands*] Of course, my
writings met with more enthusiasm in Prague.

ELIZABETH   [*Turning to face him*] Then why did
you come back?

CAMPION   I was needed.

ELIZABETH   To make rebellion?

CAMPION   To say Masses and hear confessions.
To minister to those persecuted for their Faith's
sake.

ELIZABETH   [*Convinced*] You do not sound like a
traitor.

CAMPION   Those who say I am do themselves
much greater mischief than they do me. Whatever must be done, Majesty, never believe
Edmund Campion was a traitor.

ELIZABETH   [*Businesslike*] "Whatever must be done"
is up to you, Edmund. Your only fault, so far
as I can see it, is an obstinate papism.

CAMPION   Which is my greatest glory.

ELIZABETH   [*Increasingly desperate; gesturing at the dungeon walls*] Here's your 'glory', Edmund. The Salt Tower. [*Shudders*] It's cold.

CAMPION   Her Majesty's presence brings warmth enough. [*Shivers himself*] Though in truth a small coal fire would not be unwelcome. There is a way.

ELIZABETH   [*Grasping at it*] What way?

CAMPION   [*To himself*] Out of our . . . difficulty.

ELIZABETH   Yes? What?

CAMPION   [*To himself*] It would take great bravery.

ELIZABETH   [*Encouragingly*] Of which you are capable. That we know. [*Laughing*] This merry dance you've led Walsingham's pursuivants this past year. All England knows of Edmund Campion's courage.

CAMPION   It is your bravery I speak of.

ELIZABETH   [*Wary*] Careful.

CAMPION   [*Pouncing*] You were once of the old Faith, a faith many good Englishmen believed worthy enough to die for.

ELIZABETH   [*Exploding*] Die is exactly what would happen to me if I embraced such an . . . amazing proposal. [*Furiously*] What arrant, impudent, outrageous, prideful . . . I can see your body's been broken—against my orders—but now I see your brain is broken as well. To suggest that, that, *we* . . . [*Sputtering*]

CAMPION   Open your heart to God?

ELIZABETH   [*Bitterly*] You are presumptuous, sir.

CAMPION   [*Angry*] You were born a Protestant. Then when your sister Mary became queen, you took up the Catholic Faith. Then when you became queen you re-embraced your Protestant religion. Tell me, lady, what is it you *believe*?

ELIZABETH   I believe in England.

CAMPION   [*Nods*] Yes. You do.

ELIZABETH   I don't want your death, Edmund. [*She's rehearsed this*] We are prepared to forgive your ingratitude, even to welcome you back into our favor. You would have preferment and position commensurate with your talents.

CAMPION   And, in return, I must agree—merely —to renounce my Faith.

ELIZABETH   Only in public.

CAMPION   [*Ironically*] Only in public.

ELIZABETH   What you believe, privately, is of no consequence to us.

CAMPION   [*With bitter mirth*] If a man say one thing
in public, then afterward beg God to understand that he was only doing it for convenience,
God might wonder at the quality of his fidelity.

ELIZABETH   [*Hotly*] You dare speak to me of
fidelity! You, who spurned our friendship and
fled to the court of [*Spits it out*] Prague!

CAMPION   [*Imploring her*] If I have sinned against
you, Majesty, it was pride in thinking myself
ever worthy of your friendship.

ELIZABETH   Then do you also pride yourself in
thinking that God desires your death?

CAMPION   [*Momentarily at a loss*] He desires that
we die to the world, so that we may be reborn
into his.

ELIZABETH   I will not trifle with you. I ask you
now, directly: Do you acknowledge me as
your lawful Queen?

CAMPION   I do.

ELIZABETH   And does the Bishop of Rome have
the power lawfully to depose me?

CAMPION   [*Long pause*] It is not for me to say.

ELIZABETH   [*Hotly*] Then *for whom* is it to say?

CAMPION   [*Trapped*] It is a matter between Her

Majesty and the Holy Father, not for a Jesuit priest.

ELIZABETH   Then tell me this, Jesuit priest: What would you do if the Pope sent an army to depose me? [*Venomously*] What *then*?

CAMPION   [*Slowly*] I would do as God gives me grace to do.

ELIZABETH   [*Pleading*] I'm trying to save you.

CAMPION   I know that.

ELIZABETH   Then help me! [*Desperate*] This is ridiculous. There *is* a way.

CAMPION   [*Shaking his head*] Not that one.

ELIZABETH   [*As close to begging as she comes*] You would not have to abjure your Faith publicly. Nor make *any* public statement. You would have only to attend the Anglican service.

CAMPION   Her Majesty's Catholic subjects are forbidden to attend.

ELIZABETH   You're different.

CAMPION   [*Smiling at her miscomprehension*] No. I'm their *priest*.

ELIZABETH   Attend it once. Just once.

CAMPION   And destroy everything?

ELIZABETH   [*Incredulous*] You won't go—*once*? I must say, you repose extraordinary power in one Anglican service.

CAMPION   A man has only one soul.

ELIZABETH   Your soul doesn't interest me. Your life does.

CAMPION   That I *can* give you. And if it win you over, I give it to you freely, with both hands.

ELIZABETH   [*For a moment it looks as though she will give in*] I don't want it. [*She gets up and walks to the edge of the stage*] You confuse stubbornness with sanctity. It is up to you whether we will meet again.

[*She exits. Lights down.*]

Scene Eleven

Westminster Hall. Day. The stage is dark.

VOICE OF THE QUEEN'S COUNSEL   [*Reading the indictment*] The Crown accuses you, Edmund Campion, of meeting with William Allen and other persons at Rheims and at Rome on March 31 and April 30, in the year fifteen hundred eighty, to form a conspiracy to murder the High and Mighty Lady, the Princess Elizabeth, Queen of England, Ireland, and all her dominions.

[*As the lights go up, Cecil is at his writing desk, upper stage, left. The Lord Chief Justice is at center, upper stage. Campion is on a stool halfway up the stairs—the "dock". The Queen's Counsel is at a podium, lower stage, left. The jury is on benches immediately in front of the audience.*]

LORD CHIEF JUSTICE   How do you plead to the charges, Mr. Campion?

[*Campion struggles to his feet.*]

CAMPION   My Lord Chief Justice. I protest before God and his holy angels, before heaven and earth—and this court—that I am innocent of this vile indictment. [*Collapses into chair*] It cannot be possible to find a jury in this city so wicked they would find me guilty.

LORD CHIEF JUSTICE   Administer the oath, bailiff.

[*The Bailiff goes to Campion with a Bible and holds it out to him. Campion can't raise his hand to place it on the Bible. Murmurs.*]

LORD CHIEF JUSTICE   [*Embarrassed*] Assist him.

BAILIFF   Do you swear before God Almighty that the testimony you shall give shall be the truth and only the truth?

CAMPION   [*Robustly*] I do, by Almighty God.

QUEEN'S COUNSEL   [*Rising, addressing the galleries above*] Gentlemen of the jury, well you know that the greatest enemy of the realm is the Bishop of Rome, anti-Christ and so-called Pope, self-confessed scourge of the gospel. The prisoner has lived abroad on that Pope's bounty and came into his former country as an agent of Rome, to commit great mischief and foul deeds.

CAMPION   [*Amused*] Is the Queen's counsel here in the capacity of orator?

[*Laughter from the jury.*]

LORD CHIEF JUSTICE   [*Gaveling*] Silence!

CAMPION   Or to submit evidence? At least he's made it clear I've been brought here on account of my religion.

QUEEN'S COUNSEL   My lord!

CAMPION   Be the crime but in trifles, the law has its passage. Be the crime but a half-penny, *witnesses* are produced.

[*Murmuring.*]

LORD CHIEF JUSTICE   Mr. Campion, the Queen's counsel has no intent other than duty to Her Majesty.

CAMPION   No doubt. But his duty to Her Majesty does not dignify a charge of treason. In the Tower I was offered my liberty if I would abjure the Pope, not King Philip of Spain. There is *my* proof.

[*Loud murmuring. Gavelings.*]

LORD CHIEF JUSTICE   Proceed, Counsel.

QUEEN'S COUNSEL   I call Norton, the Queen's commissioner.

[*Murmurs: "The rackmaster". Norton enters.*]

BAILIFF   Do you swear before God Almighty that the testimony you shall give shall be the truth and only the truth?

NORTON   I do.

QUEEN'S COUNSEL   You know the prisoner?

NORTON   [*Looks at Campion a bit uneasily*] Yes. He has been in my care in the Tower . . . on three occasions.

QUEEN'S COUNSEL   And you examined him on the matter of the Papal Bull excommunicating the Queen?

NORTON   I did.

QUEEN'S COUNSEL   [*Not a question*] And he endorsed the Bull.

NORTON   He . . . was pressed on the matter many times, and he led me to believe that I could reasonably infer that such was the situation that, doubtless . . .

QUEEN'S COUNSEL   [*Exasperated*] He endorsed the Bull of excommunication! Didn't he, Norton?

NORTON   [*Eyes downcast*] Well, one might deduce from the circumstantial, ah, evidence, that he would be not unopposed to such an opinion.

QUEEN'S COUNSEL   [*Shouting*] Norton! Did he or did he not endorse the Bull?

NORTON   He . . . did not.

[*Loud stirring in the galleries.*]

LORD CHIEF JUSTICE   [*Gavels*] Silence!

QUEEN'S COUNSEL   [*Incredulous*] What do you mean?

NORTON   He gave no clear answer.

QUEEN'S COUNSEL   No *clear* answer?

NORTON   [*Helpless*] I am under oath.

[*Murmuring in the gallery.*]

QUEEN'S COUNSEL   I submit to the jury an oath against the Queen. [*He hands it to the foreman.*] It was found in one of the houses where the prisoner had lodged.

[*Murmuring in the gallery as the oath is passed from juror to juror.*]

CAMPION   May I see it?

[*Queen's Counsel glances at Lord Chief Justice, who nods a bit nervously. Queen's Counsel places the document in front of Campion, who reads it.*]

CAMPION   Neither is there, nor can there be, anything imagined more directly contrary to my calling than administering this or any oath. This is a naked presumption. Does this court suggest that because this was found at a place which I once visited, that I am either its author or party to it? This is not my handwriting, and its content is repugnant to me.

[*The hall is abuzz. Repeated bangings to quiet it. Queen's Counsel and Lord Chief Justice appear worried. Lord Chief Justice turns toward Cecil, who gives a nod.*]

LORD CHIEF JUSTICE Call your next witness, Counsel.

QUEEN'S COUNSEL The Crown calls George Eliot.

[*Murmurs. More gaveling. Eliot enters. Looks taken aback by the sight of Campion.*]

BAILIFF Do you swear before Almighty God that the testimony you give shall be the truth and only the truth?

ELIOT [*It comes out a hiss*] Yes.

QUEEN'S COUNSEL [*Crisply*] Mr. Eliot, did the prisoner advocate the violent overthrow of Her Majesty the Queen in your presence?

ELIOT He did.

QUEEN'S COUNSEL Describe the incident.

ELIOT I caught him saying a Mass at Lyford Grange, the home of a Mr. Yates. [*Greasily*] I was pleased to be of assistance to Her Majesty's government in that regard by virtue of—

QUEEN'S COUNSEL [*Sharply*] Yes, yes, yes, yes.

The Crown is grateful. Now exactly what did the prisoner say?

ELIOT   [*Carefully*] He spoke of "a great day" that was shortly to come.

QUEEN'S COUNSEL   [*Cutting him off and practically shouting in triumph*] So! What could be more manifest? The great day is threatened, comfortable to them and terrible to us. And what day should that be, but when the Pope, the King of Spain, and the Duke of Florence invade this realm?

CAMPION   [*Earnest*] The great day I spoke of was the Day of Judgment. Every Protestant in every pulpit speaks of this, when the terrible Judge of us all shall try every man. *That* is the great day I threatened. And this man knows it.
      My lord, may *I* question the witness?

LORD CHIEF JUSTICE   [*Reluctantly*] You have that right.

CAMPION   Mr. Eliot, have we not met before?

ELIOT   I shouldn't think so.

CAMPION   In the Low Countries, perhaps? [*Eliot squirms*] Yes, at the English College in Douai. Were you not one of Doctor Allen's seminarians? *Briefly*?

ELIOT   It could not have been me.

CAMPION   Strange. I would remember a man like you. Tell me, did you not subsequently have some legal difficulty, sir? A murder?

ELIOT   [*Hotly*] I was acquitted of that.

CAMPION   You mean, the Earl of Leicester had your sentence commuted. But was there not another conviction?

QUEEN'S COUNSEL   I object, my lord!

LORD CHIEF JUSTICE   It is not for you to question the credibility of Her Majesty's witnesses, Mr. Campion.

CAMPION   Forgive me, my lord. I was laboring under the misconception that Her Majesty's court followed established legal procedure. [*To Eliot*] Then I will not trouble you on the matter of your conviction for rape, Mr. Eliot.

[*Eliot gets up and charges Campion. The bailiff intercepts him. The jury is shouting; the Lord Chief Justice is gaveling frantically and looking at Cecil, who is glowering.*]

LORD CHIEF JUSTICE   Another outburst like that, Mr. Eliot, and I'll have you chained to that chair. Do you understand?

[*Eliot sullenly takes his seat again.*]

QUEEN'S COUNSEL   [*This has all been scripted*] Now,

what *else* did the accused say when you ob-
served him at his blasphemous Mass, Eliot?

ELIOT   [*Precisely*] He said that the Pope of Rome
would grant special dispensation to any man
who would take the life of Elizabeth, Queen of
England.

CAMPION   [*Quietly, more in sadness than anger*] Oh,
Judas.

[*Courtroom explodes. Gaveling.*]

LORD CHIEF JUSTICE   You may step down, Mr.
Eliot. [*He looks at Cecil, who appears satisfied*]
Mr. Campion, will you speak to the jury on
your own behalf?

CAMPION   [*Rising*] I am accused of a great evil and
impleaded to the death. [*Holds out a bent arm in
the direction of Eliot; quietly*] But can you believe
that *he* has told you the truth? A man who has
betrayed both God and man and has *nothing* left
to swear by?
    [*To the Lord Chief Justice*] Is *this* the man you've
hired to hang me? I would have hoped Her
Majesty's government could have found better.
    [*To the jury*] I have no whither but to your
consciences. Remember how dear are the innocent to God. [*Gravely*] And at what price he
holds men's blood. My life is in your hands.

LORD CHIEF JUSTICE   The jury will consider its

verdict. [*Brief pause; he leans forward menacingly*]
So, *has* the jury considered its verdict?

FOREMAN   We have, my lord. [*Slight pause*] We
find the accused . . .

[*The foreman doesn't finish.*]

LORD CHIEF JUSTICE   [*Seething*] *Well?*

FOREMAN   [*Reluctantly*] Guilty. Of treason.

[*Murmuring. Gaveling. Glances between Cecil and
the Lord Chief Justice.*]

LORD CHIEF JUSTICE   Edmund Campion, do you
know of any reason why sentence of death
should not be passed upon you?

CAMPION   [*Rises with difficulty; very calm*] It was
not my death I ever feared. I knew that I was
never lord of my own life and therefore could
not be responsible for my death. All I can say to
you is, if my religion makes me a traitor, then I
am worthy to be condemned. Otherwise I am,
and have always been, as good a subject as the
Queen ever had.
   [*Voice rising*] But in condemning me, you
condemn *all* your own ancestors, all the ancient
priests, bishops, and kings, all that was once the
glory of England, the island of saints, and the
most devoted child of the See of Peter.
   For what have I taught, however you may
qualify it with the odious name of treason, that

they did not teach? To be condemned with them, by their degenerate descendants, is both gladness and Victory to me.

[*He slumps in his seat*] God lives. Posterity will live, and their judgment is not so liable to corruption as that of those who are now going to sentence me to die.

[*Murmurs.*]

LORD CHIEF JUSTICE [*To the galleries*] Silence!
Edmund Campion, you must go to the place from whence you came, there to remain until you shall be drawn through the open city of London upon hurdles to the place of execution, and there be hanged and let down alive, and your privy parts cut off, and your entrails taken out and burnt in your sight; then your head cut off and your body divided into four parts, to be disposed of at Her Majesty's pleasure. And God have mercy on your soul.

CAMPION Amen!

[*Lights down.*]

Scene Twelve

Campion*'s cell in the Tower.* Campion *on his knees, praying.* Jailer *enters.*

JAILER   Visitor.

[*George Eliot enters. Jailer remains behind, observing the scene.*]

CAMPION   [*Surprised*] You.

ELIOT   [*Nervous, lying*] I . . . I didn't know they would take it this far. I thought it would mean only prison.

CAMPION   [*With humor*] I'm surprised a man of your experience would have made that assumption.

ELIOT   Still. I'm sorry.

CAMPION   If you are truly sorry, then make your confession. I will absolve your sin.

ELIOT   You would?

CAMPION   But *large penance* thou must have!

ELIOT   [*Bursts*] Your Catholics are after me! Ever since that fishwife on the road from Lyford called me "Judas". Now everyone's calling me that!

CAMPION   [*Ironically*] Oh?

ELIOT   You yourself called me that—at the trial.

CAMPION   Sorry. Strain of the moment.

ELIOT   [*Missing it; babbling*] I was in a difficult position.

CAMPION   Oh, I'm sure.

ELIOT   The Marshallsea prison's no treat, you know. People ought to be more understanding. Now I'm not safe anywhere. I wouldn't be surprised if your followers are planning to kill me.

CAMPION   You are much deceived, Mr. Eliot. No good Catholic would push his detestation of you to revenge.

ELIOT   It's not the *good* Catholics I'm worried about.

[*Campion stares at him a moment.*]

CAMPION   I can recommend you to a certain duke in Germany. You could live there under his protection, in perfect safety.

ELIOT   You would?

CAMPION   I'll see to it. You'll receive instructions.

ELIOT [*Slightly shocked*] Well . . . thank you, then. [*Anxious to leave*] Good day.

[*Eliot starts out.*]

CAMPION And confession?

ELIOT Oh . . . yes . . . that.

CAMPION [*With pity*] In Germany.

[*Eliot exits. The Jailer drops to his knees.*]

JAILER God's mercy, forgive me, Father!

[*Campion reaches out with one arm as if to brush the sobbing Jailer's cheek.*]

Scene Thirteen

Richmond Palace. Elizabeth *enters, upper stage. She is holding a rolled-up piece of foolscap in one hand. After a moment* Leicester *enters briskly, bows.*

LEICESTER   You sent for me, Majesty.

ELIZABETH   You are to attend the execution to-morrow.

LEICESTER   Yes, Ma'am.

ELIZABETH   Take this. [*He accepts the foolscap*] It is a pardon. Tell him [*She seems to be struggling to suppress emotion*] if he will assent to our terms, it is not too late. Even now.

[*Leicester bows, begins to exit.*]

ELIZABETH   Robin!

LEICESTER   Majesty?

ELIZABETH   [*A cry from her soul*] Make him understand!

[*He bows and exits. Elizabeth walks slowly to opposite stage and exits.*]

Scene Fourteen

Tyburn gallows. Day. Sound of a crowd. Lights up. Guards take Campion *from his cell to the edge of stage.* Cecil *and* Walsingham *are there, looking on grimly. Drunken townspeople, wenches.* Doctor Charke. *In midprocession the* Young Man *breaks through crowd and wipes* Campion's *face. He is pushed back by guards. He reaches the foot of the stairs.* Leicester *approaches with the pardon and silently offers it to him.* Campion *shakes his head. The executioner takes him up the stairs, places* Campion *center, then stands to one side, producing an ugly knife, which he whets.*

CAMPION [*Cheerfully*] God save you all! God bless you and make you good Catholics!

CHARKE [*Shouting*] *Now* will you acknowledge justification by faith alone?

CAMPION *Spectaculum facti sumus Deo, angelis et hominibus.*

MAN [*Laughing*] Such elegant phrasing!

CAMPION They are the words of Saint Paul: We are made a spectacle unto God, unto his angels and unto men, verified this day in me.

WENCH   You shall be a greater spectacle yet, Jesuit!
[*Spits*]

[*Laughter and jeering.*]

MAN   Confess your treason!

CAMPION   [*Shaking his head*] I am innocent of that.
Bear witness.

MAN   In your Catholicism, *all* treason is con-
tained.

CAMPION   My Lord, I am a Catholic man and a
priest. In that Faith I have lived, and in that
Faith I am about to die. You have what you
desire. Now have patience and suffer me to
discharge my conscience.

ALL   [*Together, tauntingly, amid laughter*] No more
speeches!
Where's your invasion now?
What about the Bull?
Traitor!
Death!

CAMPION   *Confiteor Deo, omnipotenti et vobis, fratres,
quia peccavi—*

CHARKE   Pray in English!

CAMPION   I pray in a language he understands
well.

LEICESTER [*Waving pardon*] Will you not ask the
Queen's forgiveness?

CAMPION [*Pauses*] I wish the Queen a long and
quiet reign, with all prosperity.

LEICESTER [*Softer, but insistent*] Will you not ask
the Queen's forgiveness?

CAMPION [*Pauses. Appears to waver. Then, with all
his heart*] How have I offended the Queen?

[*The executioner places the noose around his neck.
With difficulty but great dignity, Campion makes
his final sign of the Cross. Lights down until there is
only a spotlight on him; then black.*]

Scene Fifteen

Court music. The garden outside Richmond Palace. Early evening. Faint light. Elizabeth *enters, lower stage, reading a book. Then a spotlight on* Campion, *upper stage, to one side of where he hanged. She stops, as in a reverie, eyes fixed in the distance. Spotlights on both. Music builds.*

CAMPION [*Benign; very slowly*] But if these my offers be refused, and my endeavors can take no place, and I, having run thousands of miles to do you good, shall be rewarded with rigor, I have no more to say but to recommend your case and mine to Almighty God, the Searcher of Hearts, who sends us His Grace and sets us at accord before the day of payment, to the end we may at last be friends in heaven, when all injuries shall be forgotten.

[*Lights gradually down.*]

The End

APPENDIX

Additional Director's Notes

1. ACT ONE, SCENE 2. (p. 32) At opening of the scene you may want to stage music, dancing, a song, juggling, a fool, etc., *before* the Queen's entrance as well.

2. THROUGHOUT, as a question of historical accuracy, the use of "Your Majesty" did not begin until well after Elizabeth's reign. She was probably called "Your Highness" or "Your Royal Highness". Given today's usage, however, we felt it would be easier to use "Majesty". Do as you wish.

3. ACT TWO, SCENE 9. (p. 124) Street singer's scene. This is a good opportunity to develop a street dance (in contrast with the court dances) with the minor players, using more robust music and repeats of the song, if time and other production constraints permit. If not, feel free to cut either or both of the first two verses.

Campion's Brag

RIGHT HONOURABLE:

Whereas I have come out of Germanie and Boëmeland, being sent by my Superiors, and adventured myself into this noble Realm, my deare Countrie, for the glorie of God and benefit of souls, I thought it like enough that, in this busie watchful and suspicious worlde, I should either sooner or later be intercepted and stopped of my course. Wherefore, providing for all events, and uncertaine what may become of me, when God shall haply deliver my body into durance, I supposed it needful to put this writing in a readiness, desiringe your good Lordships to give it ye reading, for to know my cause. This doing I trust I shall ease you of some labour. For that which otherwise you must have sought for by practice of wit, I do now lay into your hands by plaine confession. And to ye intent that the whole matter may be

Text taken from *Ten Reasons Proposed to His Adversaries for Disputation in the Name of the Faith and Presented to the Illustrious Members of Our Universities* by Edmund Campion (St. Louis: B. Herder, 1914).

conceived in order, and so the better both understood and remembered, I make thereof these ix
points or articles, directly, truly and resolutely
opening my full enterprise and purpose.

i. I confesse that I am (albeit unworthie) a priest
of ye Catholike Church, and through ye great
mercie of God vowed now these viii years into the
Religion of the Societie of Jhesus. Hereby I have
taken upon me a special kind of warfare under
the banner of obedience, and eke resigned all my
interest or possibilitie of wealth, honour, pleasure,
and other worldlie felicitie.

ii. At the voice of our General Provost, which
is to me a warrant from heaven, and Oracle of
Christ, I tooke my voyage from Prage to Rome
(where our said General Father is always resident)
and from Rome to England, as I might and would
have done joyously into any part of Christendome
or Heathenesse, had I been thereto assigned.

iii. My charge is, of free cost to preach the
Gospel, to minister the Sacraments, to instruct the
simple, to reforme sinners, to confute errors—in
brief, to crie alarme spiritual against foul vice
and proud ignorance, wherewith many my dear
Countrymen are abused.

iv. I never had mind, and am strictly forbidden
by our Father that sent me, to deal in any respect
with matter of State or Policy of this realm, as

things which appertain not to my vocation, and from which I do gladly restrain and sequester my thoughts.

v. I do ask, to the glory of God, with all humility, and under your correction, iii sortes of indifferent and quiet audiences: *the first* before your Honours, wherein I will discourse of religion, so far as it toucheth the common weale and your nobilities: *the second*, whereof I make more account, before the Doctors and Masters and chosen men of both Universities, wherein I undertake to avow the faith of our Catholike Church by proofs innumerable, Scriptures, Councils, Fathers, History, natural and moral reasons: *the third* before the lawyers, spiritual and temporal, wherein I will justify the said faith by the common wisdom of the laws standing yet in force and practice.

vi. I would be loth to speak anything that might sound of any insolent brag or challenge, especially being now as a dead man to this world and willing to put my head under every man's foot, and to kiss the ground they tread upon. Yet have I such a courage in avouching the Majesty of Jhesus my King, and such affiance in his gracious favour, and such assurance in my quarrel, and my evidence so impregnable, and because I know perfectly that no one Protestant, nor all the Protestants living, nor any sect of our adversaries (howsoever they face men down in pulpits, and overrule us in their kingdom of grammarians and unlearned ears)[1] can maintain their doctrine in disputation. I am to sue most humbly and instantly for the combat with all and every of them, and the most principal that may be found: protesting that in this trial the better furnished they come, the better welcome they shall be.

vii. And because it hath pleased God to enrich the Queen my Sovereign Ladye with notable gifts of nature, learning, and princely education, I do verily trust that—if her Highness would vouchsafe her royal person and good attention to such a conference as, in the ii part of my fifth article I have motioned, or to a few sermons, which in her or your hearing I am to utter,—such manifest and fair light by good method and plain dealing may be cast upon these controversies, that possibly her zeal of truth and love of her people shall incline her noble Grace to disfavour some proceedings hurtful to the Realm, and procure towards us oppressed more equitie.

viii. Moreover I doubt not but you her Highness' Council being of such wisdom and discreet in cases most important, when you shall have heard these questions of religion opened faithfully, which many

---

[1] The meaning is—"The ministers tyrannize over us, as if we were a kingdom of unlearned schoolboys listening to a teacher of grammar."

times by our adversaries are huddled up and con-
founded, will see upon what substantial grounds
our Catholike Faith is builded, how feeble that
side is which by sway of the time prevaileth against
us, and so at last for your own souls, and for many
thousand souls that depend upon your government,
will discountenance error when it is bewrayed,
and hearken to those who would spend the best
blood in their bodies for your salvation. Many
innocent hands are lifted up to heaven for you
daily by those English students, whose posteritie
shall never die, which beyond seas gathering virtue and sufficient knowledge for the purpose, are
determined never to give you over, but either to
win you heaven, or to die upon your pikes. And
touching our Societie be it known to you that we
have made a league—all the Jesuits in the world,
whose succession and multitude must overreach
all the practices of England—cheerfully to carry
the cross you shall lay upon us, and never to
despair your recovery, while we have a man left to
enjoy your Tyburn, or to be racked with your
torments, or consumed with your prisons. The
expense is reckoned, the enterprise is begun; it is
of God, it cannot be withstood. So the faith was
planted: so it must be restored.

ix. If these my offers be refused, and my en-
deavours can take no place, and I, having run
thousands of miles to do you good, shall be re-

warded with rigour, I have no more to say but to recommend your case and mine to Almightie God, the Searcher of Hearts, who send us His grace, and set us at accord before the day of payment, to the end we may at last be friends in heaven, when all injuries shall be forgotten.

Chronology

1533 Princess Elizabeth born to Henry VIII and Anne Boleyn.

1534 Establishment of the Anglican church separate from Rome with Henry as its head; Henry excommunicated by the Pope.

1535 Thomas More and John Fisher executed for refusing the Oath of Supremacy.

1540 Edmund Campion born to a Catholic bookseller's family in London.

1547 Henry dies; Edward VI ascends the throne.

1553 Edward dies; after the suppression of Lady Jane Grey's usurpation, Mary becomes queen, and Roman Catholicism is restored; on a procession through London Queen Mary hears the thirteen-year-old Campion, a student at Christ's Hospital, speak in Latin; Elizabeth is also present.

1555 Campion goes up to the newly founded St. John's College, Oxford.

1557 Campion, not yet eighteen, made a Senior Fellow.

1558   Mary dies; Elizabeth, after affirming her Catholicism, takes the throne. She immediately restores the Protestant state religion.

1560   Edmund Campion takes his B.A. at Oxford.

1566   Elizabeth visits Oxford and hears Campion speak; calls him to court under the Earl of Leicester's patronage.

1568   Campion ordained as Dean in the Anglican church.

1569   Rather than preach against the Pope, Campion leaves Oxford.

1570   Campion settles in Dublin and writes his *History of Ireland*.

1572   Campion leaves Ireland during the Stukeley arrests, passes through England in disguise and makes his way to the English College at Douai in France.

1573   Campion takes his Bachelor of Theology; leaves Douai for Rome to seek admission into the Society of Jesus; travels to Prague to begin his novitiate.

1574   Appointed Professor of Rhetoric in Prague; becomes Playwright to the Holy Roman Emperor.

1578   Campion ordained to the priesthood.

1580   Campion recalled to Rome; enters England in disguise as part of the Jesuit Mission to minister to the remaining Catholics; preaches in London and around the countryside.

1581   After many attempts to find him Campion is finally betrayed in June and brought to the Tower; meets with Elizabeth; is tortured three times, examined and, refusing to submit, tried on November 14; hanged, drawn, and quartered at Tyburn on December 1.

1588   Defeat of the Spanish Armada.

1603   Elizabeth dies; James I ascends the throne.

1970   Edmund Campion is canonized on October 25.

1981   Pope John Paul II visits England, the first Pope to do so in over 500 years, and prays in the Cathedral with the Archbishop of Canterbury.

Bibliography

We would like to thank Josephine Howell, Georgina Stonor, and Ellis Wasson for their early help and advice as we began our research into the period.

Allen, Cardinal. *Martyrdom of Father Campion and his Companions*. London: Burns & Oates, 1905.

Black, J. B. *The Reign of Elizabeth*. Oxford U. Press, 1984.

Bolt, Robert. *A Man for All Seasons*. New York: Vintage, 1960.

Camm, Dom Bede. *The English Martyrs*. Cambridge: W. Heffer & Sons, 1929.

Campion, Edmund. *History of Ireland*.

———. *Ten Reasons*. London: Manressa Press, 1914.

Caraman, Philip. *The Other Face: Catholic Life under Elizabeth I*. London: Longmans, 1960.

Challoner, Bishop. *Memories of the Missionary Priests*.

Dickens, A. G. *The English Reformation*. London: B. T. Batsford, 1964.

Dymoke, J. *A Kind of Warfare*. Dobson, 1981.

Guiney, L. I. *Blessed Edmund Campion*. London: Burns Oates & Washbourne, 1930.

Mathew, David. *Catholicism in England*. London: Longmans Green, 1936.

Miller, J. *Popery and Politics in England, 1660–1680*. Cambridge University Press, 1973.

Neale, J. E. *Queen Elizabeth I*. St. Martin, 1959.

Persons, Robert, S.J. *On the Life and Martyrdom of Father Edmund Campion*.

Rowse, A. L. *England of Elizabeth*. University of Wisconsin, 1958.

Simpson, Richard. *Edmund Campion*. London: Williams and Norgate, 1867.

Trial of Campion and his Companions. Cobbett's *State Trials*, 1809.

A True Report of the Disputation. A. Nowell & W. Daye, 1583.

Waugh, Evelyn. *Edmund Campion*. London: Hollis & Carter, 1947.